Impact
Organizing Method

NO ONE WANTS TO BE OWNED BY THE THINGS THEY OWN.

So why are we drowning in stuff?

Whether you're starting a new household, trying to wrangle a house that's already full, or looking for something less hectic, it's time to start controlling your stuff so it stops controlling you. Are you ready to conquer the clutter?

With professional Organizing Expert Kammie Lisenby's Impact Organizing Method, you can transform your home, your family, and your health by changing your relationship with your possessions. In this easy, step-by-step guide, Kammie shows how simple, everyday changes can open your heart to a life of functional freedom.

KAMMIE LISENBY

Impact Organizing Method™

The Experts' Proven Method to
Transform & Declutter Your Life
for Same-Day Results

Copyright © 2020 Kammie Lisenby
Kindle Edition
ISBN: 978-1-698370-61-3

All rights reserved. No part of this publication may be reproduced, distributed or transmitted in any form or by any means, or stored in a database or retrieval system, without the prior written permission of the publisher.

Titles may be purchased in bulk for educational, business fundraising, or sales promotional use. For more information, please email info@organizingexperts.com.

LIMITS OF LIABILITY/DISCLAIMER OF WARRANTY:

The author and publisher of this book have used their best efforts in preparing this material. The author and publisher disclaim any warranties (expressed or implied), or merchantability for any particular purpose. The author and publisher shall in no event be held liable for any loss or other damages, including, but not limited to special, incidental, consequential, or other damages. The information presented in this publication is compiled from sources believed to be accurate at the time of printing, however, the publisher assumes no responsibility for errors or omissions. The information in this publication is not intended to replace or substitute professional advice. The author and publisher specifically disclaim any liability, loss, or risk that is incurred as a consequence, directly or indirectly, of the use and application of any of the contents of this information.

The inclusion of website addresses in this book does not constitute an endorsement by or associate the author with such sites or the content, products, advertising or other materials presented.

Library of Congress Cataloging-in-Publication Date

Lisenby, Kammie.
Impact Organizing Method: The experts' proven method to transform and declutter your life for same-day results / Kammie Lisenby
https://www.organizingexperts.com/
ISBN 9781698370613

Printed in the United States of America

This book is dedicated to

Lisa Worthington Brown

I met Lisa during an organizing consultation. She was thirty-four years old when I met her and had just lost her young husband to cystic fibrosis. A few months later, she was diagnosed with stage three breast cancer while in the middle of moving.

I spent much of that year by her side, organizing and executing her bucket list (getting our first tattoos and a girls' trip to Bermuda) while making her new apartment feel like home as she underwent aggressive and experimental cancer treatment.

On August 1, 2012, Lisa beat the pain and disease when she graduated to heaven. I was fortunate enough to be able to hold her as she took her last breath. It was the greatest honor and one of the most humbling moments of my life. During our time together, she would often take my hands and, with tear-filled eyes, tell me how I'd saved her life. Lisa Worthington-Brown, you have forever made an impact on my life.

In Lisa's memory, a portion of the proceeds from this book will go to serve the Homeless Backpacks Program for Yelm Public Schools. Proceeds will also be used to provide opportunities for girls in poverty to pursue entrepreneurship and higher education so that they can make an impact in the world, just as Lisa did.

Contents

The Organizing Experts' Manifesto 1

1 | What Are You Filling Your Life With? 17

2 | How to Organize Mental Clutter 21

3 | Organized Time & When To Ask For Help 39

4 | One-Day Transformation 59

5 | The Truth About Keeping Everything in Order 79

6 | Clutter Isn't Cheap 97

7 | Tiny Home, Big Living 111

8 | Health Impacts of Clutter 117

9 | Clutter at Work 127

10 | Creating a Partnership Without Clutter 137

11 | The Closet Audit 143

12 | Taking the Next Steps 155

13 | The 21-Day Cut the Clutter Challenge 157

14 | Make an Impact 169

About The Author 173

Acknowledgements 175

Resources Recommended By The Author 177

The Organizing Experts' Manifesto

1. NO MATTER THE SIZE OR DEPTH OF THE MESS, IT CAN BE TRANSFORMED IF YOU ONLY KEEP AN OPEN HEART AND A POSITIVE MIND

2. HOME IS WHERE YOU MAKE IT

3. WE BELIEVE IN CREATING A FUN WORK LIFE THAT WE LOVE AND DOESN'T FEEL LIKE WORK

4. PUT THE SAFETY AND WELL-BEING OF OUR EMPLOYEES BEFORE PROFITS

5. IN FLEXIBILITY IN OUR SCHEDULING TO ENSURE THE COMFORT AND SAFETY OF BOTH EMPLOYEES AND OUR CLIENTS

6. LESS IS MORE ON MOST OCCASIONS

7. IF LIFE FEELS HEAVY, YOU SHOULD LIGHTEN YOUR LOAD

8. TRUSTING YOUR ORGANIZER ALLOWS FOR GREATER TRANSFORMATION

9. YOUR ENVIRONMENT SHOULD BE FILLED WITH THE THINGS THAT BRING YOU COMFORT, LAUGHTER, AND CREATIVITY

10. YOU CAN BLOOM WHEREVER YOU ARE PLANTED, BUT YOU MAY HAVE TO PICK SOME DEEP-ROOTED WEEDS FROM YOUR GARDEN

11. IN COLLECTING MOMENTS, NOT THINGS

12. WITH THE RIGHT METHOD AND A LITTLE HARD WORK, WE CAN CHANGE THE WORLD ONE DISORGANIZED SPACE AT A TIME

13. OUR "CARE KITS" OPEN THE CONVERSATION ABOUT SEATTLE'S HOMELESS EPIDEMIC BY PUTTING OUR ONCE-LOVED ITEMS INTO THE HANDS OF THOSE WHO NEED THEM MOST

14. SOMETIMES IT HAS TO GET MESSIER BEFORE IT GETS BETTER

15. BY OWNING LESS, YOU CAN LIVE MORE

16. IF YOU DON'T LOVE IT, YOU SHOULDN'T BUY IT, WEAR IT, OR KEEP IT

Introduction

When life gets hectic, our spaces, minds, and commitments get overstuffed. We look around and don't know where to begin. Our home becomes just a house—a place we want to run away from rather than find comfort in. Everything is a project that becomes too overwhelming and gets ignored. In this book, I will break down my method that makes it simple to transform any space in a single day.

Impact Organizing takes readers who are overwhelmed with the clutter of the modern American lifestyle through a simple, step-by-step process to get more out of life by living with less. If you adopt the Impact Organizing Method, no matter what chaos in life may come your way, you can use these expert tips to transform any space in a single day and cut the clutter forever.

Making "maybe" piles for later will be a thing of the past. Impact organizing transforms our relationship with our belongings so we can learn to live for moments and not things.

A Clutter Story

Everyone has a story and attachment to the clutter that consumes our lives.

Honestly, this was the hardest part of the book for me to write. It's so deeply personal and also the most vulnerable part of my story. This is my truth I'm sharing with the world for the first time. To find courage, I looked at the people who have inspired my journey.

None of them are perfectly polished. None of them have had a straight line to success. So here it is. My truth. My family's zig-zag path. This is my clutter story.

One of my fondest memories as a child was that of my grandmother grabbing my small hand in hers and leading me through the dark, up the small, steep stairs to my bedroom. Every night at 8:44pm, she would tuck me in, kneel by my bedside and lead my bedtime prayer.

This is where my loving grandmother would fall asleep, in the small metal folding chair nestled next to the bed while I asked for God to bless every single person I'd ever met. Or thought of meeting—or wanted to meet. I was quite a dramatic child.

What's left out from this sweet scene is the chaos and the hoarding that engulfed us.

I vividly remember in our small, A-frame farmhouse—my grandmother in the dark, one hand holding her flashlight, the other hand grasping mine—as we slowly shuffled through the small path lined with waist-high piles of toys and boxes to find my bed. When Grandma pulled out her flashlight from the drawer, it always seemed like an adventure. To me, it was an exciting time I looked forward to.

As a child, you don't have the awareness to know that the mounds of boxes taking over the room hold a much deeper story. "Stuff" served as a distraction from the dysfunction we were living in.

> *"You learn to function in the dysfunction."*
> —Michele Garrison, Massage and Bodywork Specialist

    In my innocence, I created imaginary friends with the shadowed outlines my stuff reflected on the wood slats of my bedroom walls. I felt like I always had an eager audience of stuffed animals to entertain at all times. Much of my childhood was a projection of everything my family always wanted for themselves, and they worked tirelessly to provide everything they could dream for me and my growing wish-list of toys.

    I know with absolute certainty I was loved unconditionally as a child. My family, like any other, did the best they could with what they had. As I grew up, I realized I was also in a family battle that started long before I'd entered it—a battle where love was measured by possessions. "Stuff" masked the pain to convince ourselves that everything was fine. Clutter masked the chaos, hurt, addictions, and suffering in our home.

> *"As humans, we're just trying not to suffer. Period. For a person who hoards; whatever compulsion that they are giving into, or whatever ritual they are exercising each day. That is them trying not to suffer."*
> —Erica DiMiele

My Aha Moment

As a child, I was born into chaos and learned to function within my family's dysfunction. Addiction and alcoholism played a significant role in my upbringing and have forever shaped the person I've chosen to become. At nineteen years old, I was presented with two life-changing choices to make. Should I just give into the adversity of my upbringing or fight to rise above it?

When my relationship with my beautifully wild single mother become very strained, the world as I knew it turned on its axis. My emotional anchor to this earth—my compass who had always steered me north—went south. She was slipping away from me, and I felt as if I was the little cartoon baby duck that runs around asking all the farm animals, "Are you my mother? Can you help me, please?"

At the time, I felt as if the world I'd been living in was just a cruel joke. I was grasping to control any part of my old life and seeking a strong female role model to fill the impossibly large hole my mother had left behind. It was a time of internal struggle to find the rational in such an irrational situation.

I had the great fortune enough to live in the early 2000's era of The Oprah Winfrey Show, every weekday at 4pm. I devoured my "hour of power" as Oprah told ME that I could live my best life. No matter what chaos or adversity came my way, at 4pm. I religiously watched her show. Oprah's single intention to shift her show to living your best life changed my life forever. She taught me that the power is in the "letting go"—letting go of old stuff and old ways of thinking that no longer served me. I learned that life has seasons of observing and becoming—of learning to dance with the chaos rather than trying to control or escape it. She also taught me how to make peace with myself and those around me, to love my mother right where she is without judgment rather than try to change her.

Everyone you meet is doing the best they can in the moment. It's not our job to define what's best for someone else or to save them. As much as we want to believe we're superheroes with our own magic capes, you can't fight irrational situations with rational solutions. That's called chaos, and the only power we have over that is letting go.

One week, Oprah featured organizing expert Peter Walsh on her show. This particular episode was promoting his show *Clean Sweep*, where he would go into strangers' homes and completely transform their lives by organizing and decluttering. It was the first time I'd ever heard of a professional organizer.

As I watched the episode, I could feel my brain buzzing. Wait—people do this? And they get *paid* to do this? They actually like getting rid of stuff? Maybe grandma would let me practice on her.

Those questions changed everything.

I listened to the small voice in my head: Kammie, you've spent your twenties organizing small businesses.
What's the difference between that and helping someone at home?
What if we *can* create our dream environment?
What *if* this would help my grandma?
What possibilities would open up for her if she could tackle the "closed-door room?"

The Making of a Young Female Entrepreneur

One afternoon, when I was feeling undervalued and frustrated at my current job, I decided enough was enough. I promptly and professionally left my nine-to-five job on my lunch break. I wanted to live my best life just as my queen, Oprah Winfrey, had been promoting on TV.

At the time, I had no idea how to create a business, let alone how to spell the word entrepreneur. I found myself a few strong female business mentors (Thank you, Ali Brown and Marie Forleo) and made a simple Craigslist ad in 2008 with the intention to start working with anyone and everyone for one hundred dollars a day. I didn't care how many hours I worked or what the job entailed. I only wanted to make an impact in someone's life through whatever work I did. At the end of the day, all I needed was enough money for food and gas.

In 2008, at twenty-one years of age, I started a company from my dining room table in Fremont, Washington. My sole intention was to change the way we function freely in our existing spaces.

My grandma ended up being my first client. Bless her heart, she said yes!

My Papa, on the other hand—a retiree from Boeing—just about lost his damn mind. He couldn't comprehend why I would risk my steady paycheck and health benefits to be my own boss. This was his worst nightmare.

After all this time, I really don't think he understood what I did. I really believe he thought I was a house cleaner who did really well. It's partially true, I guess. I'd like to believe the profoundly deep relationships I've made with complete strangers goes a bit beyond a quick tidy session.

A few years into my business, I started appearing on our local TV station. That's when my Papa finally said, "Hey kiddo, you look good on that TV." Finally, he accepted the idea of me working for myself.

After my grandma agreed to let me help her, I started with the idea of cleaning out the backroom just enough so we could walk through it. I figured if we tackled her biggest fear first, everything after that would be easy. I was right. What started out as just a quick clean sweep of the backroom turned into a massive transformation of clearing, painting, and drywall repair with just the two of us working side by side.

Meeting Oprah Winfrey

Things really came full circle for me in 2012 when I got to meet (and hug) both Oprah Winfrey and Peter Walsh. I'll never forget when Peter jumped off the stage at the Live Your Best Life Tour in New York City to hug me. I hold these moments so close to my heart. It was a dream come true to meet my TV mentors and thank them for changing my life.

People ask me all the time what it was like meeting Oprah. I can only reply that it was amazing—absolutely amazing. She's everything I imagined and more. Her hugs are pure magic!

Transformation Through The Tears

Nearly everything we care about accomplishing comes with some level of pain. Discomfort is just part of the growing pains of moving forward. There is no comfort in change and no change in comfort.

My grandma cried a lot during our first time organizing together. She cried because she didn't want to deal with it. She cried because she was embarrassed. She cried when I coached her on which things to part with and which things to keep. Finally, she cried happy tears when we finished the "closed-door room" together.

She still remembers the Great Depression—when her mother had to break the dining room chairs to heat the house for her three small children. She is a survivor, even through an era of daunting challenges that had a lasting effect on her life. Although she retained her generational hoarding tendencies, I have great respect for her intentions. She comes from a generation of sacrifice and scarcity, and I'm living in a time of overabundance in every form.

For her, clutter provides comfort as a sort of safety net. It was emotionally hard for her to process discarding little "somethings" that could be used someday. When we were organizing together, I took great care and consideration for her process of letting go.

A reality never thought possible, that she could ever see anything other than the chaos she was living in day-to-day. To overcome that space was challenging for her emotionally and physically, but that room soon became one of her favorites in the house.

That's when I knew I was onto something truly more than just organizing. This was life changing.

Helping my grandma was the beginning of what I would later discover to be my lifelong passion and calling—helping individuals brave their way through their own "clutter stories" and step into a better, beautiful life. Right now, at this very moment, the very environment that has caused so much chaos can be the start of a new beginning.

What Is an Organizing Expert?

The Organizing Experts have helped thousands of people over the last decade declutter their homes and businesses to find purpose beyond a purchase. When people ask what I do for a living and I tell them I'm an Organizing Expert who helps people declutter their lives, they usually have one of three reactions:

- A deeply puzzled look followed by grave concern. "People actually pay you for that?" or "Oh, yeah. I've seen Hoarders. How do you do that?"

- The complete opposite reaction: "Oh my gosh, I would love to have someone like you around the house!" "My sister/friend/neighbor/mother/cousin/boss definitely needs your help!"

- My personal favorite: "You're a miracle worker!"

When my clients invite me into their home—arguably, their most intimate space—I know firsthand how hard conquering clutter can be. I know chaos very well. When people share with me how overwhelmed and embarrassed, they are about their space, I always assure them that it's nothing I haven't seen before. It's not so much about the stuff, but the story anchored to it.

My clients are busy professionals who are always blown away with my method for impact organizing. It works like magic and is a true method for how to get it done quickly. Not only does it speed up the process, but it also dramatically changes the visual look and feel of the space you're working in. Did I mention it all happens in a few hours?

Using this method can transform how your space looks and feels in just a few hours. The best part of my method is that it doesn't matter if you're on the verge of being featured on Hoarders or just in need of some quick tidying help. Using this method will make the most of your time so that you can see and feel the difference the very same day.

I'm now a consultant for professional organizers and help small business entrepreneurs and individuals get organized. I offer coaching, courses, and in-person guidance to living a life with less—less stress, less stuff, and more time to make memories.

Helping others let go is so rewarding. Each day, I help people create a shift in their homes and lives simply by getting rid and letting go of what no longer serves them. One client told me, "The feeling of letting go feels light, and the feeling of holding on to things is so heavy. When I declutter, it literally feels like a weight has been lifted off my shoulders instantly."

You know you've experienced the "magic" when you feel lighter.

It seems we spend the first half of our lives accumulating stuff and the second half getting rid of it.

Over the last decade, my team and I have discarded thousands of donated items to benefit local organizations and families. It truly is life-changing work for everyone involved. Here are some testimonials from my Seattle clients:

"This business is an investment in myself that will help my MONEY grow, rather than stuff. Get an appointment booked ASAP! You'll be happy you did!"

"They helped me turn a room that I couldn't even walk in into livable space."

"They made it easy to make reasonable decisions regarding my stuff. I am so impressed, and so is my partner. He was like, 'Where did everything go?' And I was like, 'I put it away!' My life feels so much less hectic and less stressful."

"Amazing! Outstanding! Hard-working, sensitive, and creative. The Organizing Experts were respectful and efficient. I would highly recommend them for overwhelming tasks for busy young professionals trying to set up a new home in an organized way, people downsizing from a larger home to a smaller one or

creating a shared space, or just overwhelmed by an explosion of kid or teen stuff. Avoid the hassle, the fights, and the tears!"

"They are also very trustworthy. I felt okay leaving them by themselves in my home while I ran an errand, which normally I wouldn't feel comfortable doing with people I just met! Anyhow, the end result of our work is wonderful! I have to admit that I was nervous (and a bit mortified) to have them come into my space—which after being out of commission for three years due to repeated surgeries and health stuff looked like a bomb went off—but they were so great about it and totally non-judgmental, and I needn't have worried. So relieved that I discovered them and finally took that first step! I HIGHLY, HIGHLY recommend them! And, amazingly, I'm actually looking forward to our next session! Love you guys!"

Every in-person organizing session is a very intimate process handled with care that holds the intention of what each client wants to create for their space. We have no judgment and no agenda but to make an impact on all the lives that we touch. We walk into each home and office with an open heart and mind.

Time and time again clients will say, "Wow! How did you do that so fast?"

This is the magic of the Impact Organizing Method that I share with you in detail throughout this book. I know for certain it doesn't take years to get your life organized. It starts with a shift in your mindset and collecting little "wins" of progress along the way.

If you're ready to make an impact, turn the page and let's get started!

Collect moments, not things.

PART ONE

1 | What Are You Filling Your Life With?

I've organized this book into three parts based upon my experience working with my clients over the last decade. I also know that if you're reading this, you're craving organization in your life. Throughout this book I've added impactful tips, takeaways, questions, and challenges so that you can do the real work of putting these ideas into action in your life.

The first part is dedicated to helping you:

- Understand your clutter story and how to move past it.
- Discover what living an impactful, organized life means *to you*.
- Recognize *why* it's important to live organized.
- Get past the emotional and mental clutter.
- Break down the Impact Organizing Method.
- Take the challenge of putting everything you've learned into action.

The second part is dedicated to helping you:

- organize the most important things first.

- understand what I like to call, "Top Requested Areas to Organize"
- learn from other industry experts how to get organized with your kids, how to merge households, how to organize your closet, and so much more!

The last part of this book is dedicated to answering my clients' most frequently asked questions and providing a resource guide to help you live organized and make an impact.

"We can borrow everything in life," my papa used to say. "There is no need to take possession of it. Everything must be returned when we leave this earth anyway, you know? You never see a hearse pulling a U-Haul, kid."

It's time to take a look at what you're filling your life with and explore the reason behind the collecting. Let's say you have a love affair with shoes. Having a lot of shoes may be something you take great pride in, but have you ever asked yourself *why* that is?

Only you and your therapist can dig deep enough to figure out if that *why* is destructive or enriching. I'm just the organizer. My job as an Organizing Expert is to help you contain your shoe collection.

Here's what I'm concerned with.

Do your shoes cause you stress when you're trying to find a certain pair? Do you have a system to keep them organized? Does every pair have a home? Are they mismatched and tossed in your closet?

This is the most common issue we deal with. We have all these things we love, but they can add more stress than usefulness in our lives.

"When you want something new in your life, you have to let go of the old. There won't be space for newness to exist if your life is full of old energy. I encourage my clients to declutter their

physical space, their calendars, their minds, etc. It creates an opening for the Universe to drop in magic, miracles and new energy."
—Bri Seeley, Permission to Leap

By no means am I telling you how many pairs of shoes to own. I have created shoe *rooms* for clients who own hundreds of pairs. However, when you're bringing them into your home and they're causing more stress than happiness, your shoes have become a problem. As much as you love them, more shoes will only bring more chaos.

Shouldn't we be focusing on filling your life with happiness?

I love the saying "Collect moments, not things." We should be doing that every day. What if we adorned our life with new memories and not things? Each new day is an opportunity to do something different than yesterday. Think differently. Choose differently. Be a better version of yourself. Intend to collect moments of goodness and make beautiful memories with your friends and family. These will be the makings of your lifetime.

Memories that make you giggle or smile are an appreciating asset. They are worth hoarding and investing in. Good memories only get sweeter with time. You'll never regret making a memory with those you love.

The choice to cut clutter from our lives is the first step toward living with less. This allows, us to make an impact on the world around and within us.

2 | How to Organize Mental Clutter

Thoughts are like children racing out of the classroom to recess. The bell rings (our morning alarm clock), and the kids (thoughts) shove each other at the same time, crowding and pushing their way to the front door trying to reach the playground of life. You are the playground supervisor of your thoughts. Your job is to kindly and lovingly walk the playground (your mind), observing and rewarding children who are displaying acts of kindness (good thoughts) and correcting kids who need more guidance (negative thoughts).

"It's important to be careful what you allow into your mind because it can get cluttered. There might not be room for all the positivity and all the things that you really do need to be focusing on. I realize decluttering everything in my life was actually the best thing I've ever done."
—Anny Havland of KIND TV

Brain-Dump Blueprint

When it comes to clutter, you're not alone if you're feeling overwhelmed and unsure of where to start. Often, when I first meet a client during our consultation process, the first thing they tell me is that they're so overwhelmed, they can't *think* straight. The clutter seems like so much, they have no idea where to begin.

Thoughts have a way of running amok and can cause a sense of frustration and stress if not managed. Organizing your thoughts is essential. Your mind is your internal space, and if you're feeling unsure where to start, let's begin with a brain dump.

This is a technique I acquired years ago through attending a networking event for women in business. The entrepreneur leading the group called it "mind-mapping." It's a popular technique for clearing the clutter from your mind. In my opinion, our thoughts, if not organized, can be paralyzing. Although I like the technique of mind-mapping, I prefer a more linear approach to organizing my thoughts. This is why I use brain dumping.

> "Everything is energy, and it is either positively contributing to your environment or it is stealing from you. There is stuff in your space that is, multiple times a day, stealing energetically from you. And you have the choice to move it out and get rid of it."
> —Julie Anne Jones, Direct Sales Trainer

If you're ever feeling overwhelmed by work and life in general, take five minutes to organize your thoughts using the method below.

Step 1: What's on your mind?

Take a few moments, preferably at the beginning of your day, and without editing or judgment, dump all your thoughts onto paper. Write out every single thing that's stressing you, monopolizing your thoughts, or consuming your energy. Do not worry about spelling, order, or even what that thought is. None of that matters. What *matters* is getting it out of your head and onto paper so you can see it.

If your list is a mile long, take heart. Once you have all the thoughts out of your head and onto paper, give yourself permission to delete, delegate, and tackle the items on your list.

Step 2: What can you delete?

Working with each thought on your list, ask yourself which ones you can delete. One by one, take an honest look at each item and give yourself permission to get rid of it. Can you come to terms with any of your written thoughts and feel good about deleting them? Maybe not forever, but for today, can you delete this from your mental clutter?

Notice how you feel as you move through your list. Also take notice of your challenges. Maybe you have something on your list you desperately want to let go of but aren't ready to delete. If you come to a thought that's just too overwhelming and needs attention, this is where Step 4 comes in. This just happens to be my favorite step!

> **Expert Tip:** Put a big, fat ~~strikethrough~~ through any thought you can DELETE. I like to use a red/pink pen for this step.

Step 3: What can you delegate?

What thoughts on your list would you like to delete, but simply can't? Can you delegate it instead? These pesky thoughts may need a little more supervision and attention. Perhaps there's someone you can ask to help you with this thought or task. For example, if you're struggling with cleaning or getting caught up on laundry, think of someone who could help you. Could you possibly hire someone or ask another member of your household to help out?

Think of Beyoncé. She can be the woman she is because she has an expert team of support. Organizing can be daunting and we all need a cheerleader to get us through. Heck, last time I checked, NFL cheerleaders are only making minimum wage, Help a sister out and hire one.

Sometimes, the things we feel overwhelmed by are simply nudging us to grow into the person we truly want to be. Our thoughts naturally have a protective way of limiting us for perceived safety.

While we all can't be Beyoncé, we can all ask for help right here in our own neighborhood. As you move through your brain dump, consider the tasks you could delegate to someone else to and get them off your plate and out of your mind. You never know. By reaching out to your network, you could financially or emotionally help someone who is seeking to find fulfillment in helping you.

> **Expert Tip:** I like to use a blue pen for this task and write my ideal person's name next to that specific task.

Step 4: What's top priority?

In this phase, your brain dump list should have some strike-through thoughts you've deleted and a name you've added next to the thoughts that you've delegated. This is where you can reassess your remaining thoughts/tasks and highlight your top three most important "must happen now" items. I know you may feel that everything on your list needs to happen yesterday, but I really urge you to look at what is left and only pick a few to highlight as your most important priorities.

> **Expert Tip:** Use a basic highlighter for the top three thoughts/tasks.

Step 5: Time It Out

You made it to the final step! Now, when you take a look at your brain dump, it should look like, well... A dump. I hope you have strikethrough marks, names, and highlights on your page. If so, it tells me that you're giving yourself permission to let go, get help, and make things happen. If not, it's okay. This may be a new concept for you, and you may find it hard to let go or ask anyone for help. You're not alone. Remember, getting yourself and your home organized is all about self-care. Be kind to yourself as we move to this final step in the brain dump. This step is about asking yourself, "Of all the tasks that I have, how much time will each task take?"

Some may be quick five-minute phone calls or thirty-minute tasks. Others may be a bit longer. That's okay. All I want you to do is designate a time limit in front of the written task. How long do you estimate it will take to complete the thought/task? If you're delegating the task, that's great! Now you can let the person you are delegating to know how long you think it will take. It gives you and everyone else a foundation to work with. When I'm working with clients, I always tell them how long I think each task will take. So next to each thought/task on your sheet, put the time.

I go down my list of remaining items and put a number by each one. Then, on the back of my brain dump paper, I write down my top three tasks as well as thirty-minute tasks so I know which ones to knock out first. Little wins are a big thing to celebrate. It feels so good to cross things off a list!

> Expert Tip: I go down my list of remaining items and put a number by each one. Then on the back of my brain dump paper I write out all my top three and take my 30-minute tasks and knock them out first. Little wins are a BIG thing to celebrate. It feels SO GOOD to cross things off a list!!!

Mental clutter may not have been what you had in mind when you picked up this book, but this process is the best way to start your decluttering process. I recommend you begin each day with a blank sheet of paper and give your brain some structure.

Try This Impact Challenge

Each morning take five minutes to visualize your day. A light, meditative moment for yourself. Make your bed, pick up the floor, then give yourself time to enjoy your morning before you have to take care of anyone else. Make some coffee or tea and feed your body good food.

When you're properly nourished, set a timer on your phone for ten minutes and allow your brain to dump. After you've got those thoughts out, reset the timer for five minutes and go through the items you can delete. Reset the timer once more for five minutes and go through the items you can delegate. List your top three for today and get to work!

Chicken Foot

My Papa was quite a character. One day, if I'm blessed enough, I would love to make a movie of his life. He was quite a character and very loud-mouthed. It should come as no surprise that even after his death he would have the last laugh.

I was my grandfather's primary caretaker and provided hospice care for him until his last day with us. I also was running a business, the farm, and my grandmother's sole supporter. When my grandfather passed, my life felt like I was running on autopilot just going through the motions. I had made arrangements at a local funeral home to have him cremated and placed in an urn that he specifically told me to use. As I'm rushing around the house that morning to the funeral home, I nearly forgot the urn! I knew exactly where it was because, ever since I was little, he would always point to it on the top shelf in the garage and proclaim, "One day, I'll be buried in that!"

I remember looking into that dusty thing when I was younger and running with it in my hands to my Papa.

"Ahhh! Look," I told him. "There's a dead mouse in there!"

He just smiled. "Oh. He was just keeping it warm for me."

May 18th 2016, my Papa passed away and once again, my reality shifted forever in a new direction. In the middle of the chaos that followed those blurred weeks, I ran into the garage to grab the urn off its dusty shelf, running late (of course) to bring it into the funeral home for his arrangements. As I grabbed it, I realized there was a disgusting amount of dust and cobwebs on it. I was pretty horrified that this was what I was placing my Papa in.

As tears rolled down my face, I ran into the kitchen to quickly clean it off so that I could get the funeral home on time. I was rinsing the outside when I decided to give the inside a quick cleaning, and what felt like a small hand brushed mine...

My Papa knew whoever was going to make his arrangements would have to look inside to find a petrified chicken claw. I was that lucky soul, and it scared the hell out of me. I instantly stopped crying because I was terrified. Then, I could just see him watching this all happening, and I'm sure he was in hysterics. Even in heaven, he still finds a way to have the last laugh.

When someone owns something, it was a joy for their lifetime, and it's okay if it's not yours. What matters most is that you remember their spirit during ordinary moments in the day and find new meaning and joy from what is left behind. Some days I struggle to hear my Papa's voice in my head. But when I look at that chicken foot that now sits in a mason jar on my fridge, I instantly feel his childlike humor and hear his words over me, I know that everything really will be okay.

Emotional clutter is something most of us will have to deal with at one time or another when someone we love leaves this earth. Just remember, it's not about the stuff, it's about appreciating ordinary moments.

Keep what you love and brings love into your heart. Everything else is just clutter.

What Can You Live Without?

Make a quick list of all the things you could truly live without. Sure, it will be an adjustment, but this is your challenge. Write down five things you really won't miss. I do this *all the time* in my personal and professional life. Being in a continuous state of editing is a superpower habit to adopt.

Here are some items I've recently purged.

- Cable is way too expensive and dangerous to my mental health lately. I will instantly turn into a couch potato and tune out every voice that isn't coming from my TV. I haven't had cable for over a decade, and I don't miss it one bit. Thank you, Netflix & YouTube!

- Shoes that hurt my feet. I don't know what happens in your thirties but for me, it became a lot easier to get real with myself. I love a beautiful shoe just as much as Carrie Bradshaw does, but if it hurts me, it's got to go. Getting real with myself liberated me from so much guilt. If I looked at a shoe and remembered the last time I wore it was hobbling out of a club, I knew our relationship was over. You don't need a five-inch heel to make you feel sexy. Wobbling around like a deer after ten minutes of wearing your shoes doesn't look very sexy, either. Stop the madness. Your feet will thank you.

- Scarves are something I always tease my best friend about. I've never seen a scarf collection quite like it in my life—and I've seen a lot of scarves. I always know where to find her if we go to TJ Maxx. She's either trying on sunglasses or finding that perfect scarf. Personally, I went through a few seasons with scarves. Then I realized I only wear three of them. So, I purged the rest. The new fad was chunky, blanket-type scarves, which I now love the most. I've only kept two lightweight scarves. Do you really wear all the scarves you own?

- Skirts and shorts, never again. The women in my family have always had big legs. I used to hate them, and now that I don't get to see the women in my family, I've come to love them as they are. With that being said, even at my smallest, I've never been a fan of showing my legs off. I always dread wearing shorts or skirts because I have the mermaid leg-action going on. I've kept three pencil skirts "just in case," but let's be honest, I will not wear them with excitement. I've got way too much going on to be constantly fussing and pulling that garment out of uncomfortable places. If I had to choose between pants, a dress, or a skirt, I'd pick the first two all day long. Knowing what you hate wearing makes it easier to get rid of that item.

- Coffee mugs. I'm a single gal, I do not need seventy-five coffee mugs. A hoard of coffee mugs is not trendy. While standing in line at Starbucks, skip the urge to purchase another mug just because it has a sassy quote. When going through your cupboard, pick your favorite four mugs per person in your household. If you host often, keep the extra mugs with your entertaining dinnerware.

Boxes

Amazon has been a beautiful gift of convenience over the last decade. You can pretty much get anything, anytime at the push of an "add to cart" button. In our current American culture of instant gratification and impulsive consumerism, cardboard has consumed our spaces.

Seattle is home for me, and I'm at the epicenter of Amazon's world domination. Of course, I see the cardboard-box-hoard more than the average person. I'm not blaming Amazon for anything, it's just a sign of the times. Let's be clear on that—I love me some Amazon Prime.

The number of boxes we have coming into our homes is quite possibly the most we've ever experienced. I believe we can cohabitate with cardboard boxes without them taking over our essential spaces. To tackle this cardboard box epidemic, let's break down some new habits.

Try one of these ideas.

Each time you open a box, break it down right then and there. (Don't just slice it open to see what's inside.) Take all that mess to a central drop spot in your home. Now, it's in a neat and tidy location for disposal.

If you're too lazy to break them down, try this! Throw all your open boxes into a pile in the garage. The next time you need to relieve some stress, go to your one box pile and have a stop and slice party—a safe, nonharmful stop and slice party. I had a client try this technique, and she really loved it. She told me it was a great way to relieve stress. Every Tuesday night before the trash came, she would go into the garage, turn on her favorite tunes, and go to town on breaking down boxes.

You can have fun decluttering if you allow yourself, but you have to create the space in your head and your home. Creating small spaces in our homes to simply take up space and allow ourselves moments to breathe make a world of difference.

Clutter-Free Confidence

Confidence comes from clutter-free living. This I know for sure. You no longer have to feel a daily sense of panic looking for things or worrying that other people will think less of you when you are not prepared. Taking the time to organize your brain and taking control of how you start each day gives you the confidence to be the boss of your life. Life gets crazy. If you don't have a set of positive habits in place, each day can melt into the next.

We live in an American culture that has long viewed slowing down as settling, rather than preparing. Your foundation will only stand the test of time if the prep work was done properly. What's missed by running from place to place is that life can truly be fulfilling if we open our hearts and minds. When you feel valuable, you're operating and making decisions from that place—complete confidence.

Imagine if consumption wasn't the pillar of our economy. Are we ready to see the world differently? Imagine that doing without is not considered a failure. Are we ready to simplify our lives and cut the clutter?

Are you rocking your work life but feel overwhelmed with your personal space? It's so interesting to me when clients tell me that their office is immaculate, but they're not that way at home, or vice versa. Often, it's because work has a set of guidelines, systems, and appearances that they're required to adhere to. When you get home, it's a free-for-all. Or, you're simply working so much that when you get home, you barely have enough energy left over to brush your teeth and do it all over again.

You need to keep in your mind that less is so much more. If you have less stuff, you have less to worry about and less overall stress. All those little decisions add up. The last thing you want to do in your free time is to organize your pantry. I get it.

Loving What You Have

Trusting yourself to do what's best at this moment is liberating. The confidence of simply taking the guesswork out of knowing what you own frees up not only space in your mind and environment, but also in your life. Getting your life organized overflows confidence into every area of your life.

When you have clothes that fit the body you have now, that's confidence.

When a coworker or boss asks you for something and you can find it quickly, that's confidence.

When you teach your child to emotionally detach from physical items, that's confidence.

When you know what you own and where it's kept, that's confidence.

Are you overcommitted?

Are you a busy mom rushing your kids from place to place? Close down your taxi service for a bit and see how life begins to slow down again.

Do you find yourself helping everyone and overcommitting to every opportunity that comes your way? Give yourself some breathing room from all you've overcommitted to. How can you simplify your weekly schedule of commitments? Keeping a schedule can help prevent you from overbooking yourself. With a simple schedule easily accessible (on your smartphone, for example), you can log your current obligations and stay on track.

Start saying no to more and yes to freedom. Don't get trapped by spreading yourself too thin. Make sure your commitments are in alignment with your values and long-term goals. What is something you could quit that would open space for simplicity?

Mental Mornings

The one repeating excuse most of my clients have is that they just don't have the time. I can see it in their faces and hear it in their delivery—victim mentality. I don't mean to be harsh, but when you use this line on a daily basis, it starts getting old. All of us have the same twenty-four hours in a day. You and only you are in charge of your life and your time.

You want more time in your day? Start by facing the hard truth of the matter. Shift from, "I just don't have the time" to admitting that you don't take the time. Why do this? Because now you take ownership. You're stating that you don't take the time to do something.
You know what happens next. Be honest.
Why are you not taking the time?

The mastery of living is simply knowing that you're the captain of your time. You can either choose to make it, take it, or waste it. Time has a wonderfully poetic way of making us realize what truly matters. In the end, what we choose to do with our time defines our life. One thing I loved about becoming an entrepreneur was that I could create my life on my own terms. I had a new choice of where and how to spend my time. What I quickly realized was that by creating the life of my choosing, I had to become a master of routine. I had so much time that it was all mine, and if not taken into account, this can be where many of us slip off track. Without a routine, it's all too easy to either forget or procrastinate. You don't need to be militant. Start by creating a simple morning routine.
Let's do that now.

Close your eyes for a moment and just daydream for sixty seconds about what your ideal morning would look like. Would you be in your bedroom, coffee in hand, getting ready for the day? Do you see a messy bed or a made one? Do you see clothes on the floor or in the hamper? By taking the time to breathe and visualize what you want in your mind, it becomes easier to determine the steps you need to take.

My most successful clients are those who are able and willing to make quick decisions. Learn to stop saying yes to things that don't serve you. Rather than thinking your power or confidence comes from having, I want to train your mind to feel powerful simply by being. Become alive to your life. It's okay to slow down and not be busy. Be the boss and get clutter-free confidence. Clutter is simply an accumulation of delayed decisions.

When you take a moment to slow down, look at life and prime yourself for the day. You'll start making decisions with clarity and confidence.

Distracted?

It's easy to get distracted. To make the biggest impact in the shortest amount of time, focus on what I call zones. A zone can be a specific pile, area, or room. Applying the Impact Organizing Method in each zone creates the biggest overall impact.

Take this story as an example of what can happen to your day when you try to organize without focus. Let's meet Jess.

Jess wants to organize her bedroom closet. Instead of starting with the floor, she starts with the top shelf and stumbles upon a box of old photos of her and her ex-boyfriend. She then takes this box and wonders what she should do with it.
Burn it?
Store it?
But maybe if she just takes a peek, she can see if there's something worth saving. Just one little...
No, Jess. Noooooo!
She sits on her bed going through all the memories, photos, and keepsake items in the ex-files.
It's okay. We all have or have them. Trust me, I've seen it all.
Instead of zipping through the floor clutter like she was supposed to and getting rid of any garbage, recycle, and

obvious items, she's lost precious time thinking about her ex. Now Jo is depressed and hits the kitchen for some ice cream. She calls her best girlfriend to rehash the details of why the relationship didn't work out. #OrganizingFail

    You may think it's stupid and nonessential to start with my method, but it's the fastest way to accomplish one small task and reap a huge result.

Quick Decision-Making Skills

My clients know that the faster you're able to make decisions, the more transformation we can make in a given amount of time. However, some situations can't be rushed, and they hold a lot of emotional attachment. Be kind to yourself and to others. You'll be able to move through your space with ease when you have the right mindset and are not feeling outside pressures.

Take it One Bite at a Time

My papa would often ask me silly riddles.

Papa: If a hog-and-a-half costs a dollar-and-a-half, how many hogs does it take to make five dollars?
Kammie: Eyes roll.

The words coming out of his mouth were completely ridiculous. I'm a practicing vegetarian! Who around here is going to buy a hog, anyway?
But there's one phrase that did stick with me.

Papa: Kammie, what's the fastest way to eat an elephant?"
Kammie: Another look of annoyance.
Papa: One bite at a time, honey...

Isn't it true of so many of life's challenging situations, especially if you're impatient? Personally, I would like everything to be done – yesterday. Just skip all this nonsense and get straight to the end result. The truth is, when you're feeling overwhelmed by clutter, if we can step back and just take one bite at a time our overall experience is much richer.

For some of you, you may have years of accumulated clutter. It may take days, months, or even, in my case, a few years to get everything how you'd like it. Focus on the progress, it will get done if you keep at it.
One bite at a time.

3 | Organized Time & When To Ask For Help

I often get an enormous sense of guilt and shame for not being able to balance it all. Why do we never stop to consider why we feel pressured to live this way? We are the designers, in control of how we live our lives. When feeling overwhelmed, why is it so hard to ask for help? Maybe you've never considered hiring an organizer to help you.

Here are a few indicators that it may be time to enroll some help to make an impact in your home.

- Don't have hours to dedicate to getting projects organized.
- When I have a few moments of rest, I really need to spend it with family.
- I always find myself interrupted or distracted when trying to get organized.
- It's overwhelming when there's more than one space to tackle.
- I'm not sure where exactly to put things to maximize space and function.
- I just don't have the energy to start or finish organizing.

I've had women break down in tears, overwhelmed and ashamed that they had to call an expert to help. They felt like hiring help was confessing that they couldn't do it all. Meanwhile, they're balancing a demanding career, a Pinterest-perfect house, all the latest gadgets, their families, and doing it all while looking fabulous.

The truth is, it's all too much for anyone to live up to. Even those who "have it all" seek the same thing—more time to invest in what matters most.

We also have clients who have been able to flip the script on what success means in their lives. They understand that we all have only so many hours in one given day. For these women, I've found they understand the value of their "life time." Each day they have prep time, focused time, time to share, and even time to waste. They have an ease to their lives because they've invested in getting help where they need it in order to be successful.

> "I used to be really proud of how little sleep I got, how much I was working, and overall how busy I was. But now that I'm a business owner, a mom, and a military spouse, things have changed a bit. I really don't get that much sleep, but now I am realizing it's not really a great badge to have. To be busy and burnt out all the time, it's not something to be proud of. I've learned that it's better to be able to say I got eight hours of sleep last night and I took the weekend off because I've been able to streamline and actually ask for help. I've learned you have to drop that ego and admit that you can't do everything yourself. There are times when I want to do it all myself, and then I realize that I have to be vulnerable and ask for help."
>
> —Rebekah Adams, Poppyseed Clothing

Maybe you've never thought of working with an organizer or feel it's a luxury only for the wealthy. Or maybe hiring an Organizing Expert is just what you've always dreamed of.

Either way, your life will be impacted forever by working with an expert whose sole purpose is to transform your space and allow you to spend your time focusing on things that truly matter in your life.

Yes, it's true. Finding good help you can trust can be a challenge or a bit intimidating at first. But don't give up. I believe this world is full of people who crave to make an impact! If this is something that sounds interesting to you, I'd like to walk you through our exact process of providing an in-home consultation with our clients.

This way, you can get a glimpse into how this would apply in your life and decide if working with an expert is something you want to invest in.

Our Consultation Process: Finding Trust

Impact Organizing is about creating an impact far beyond yourself. The changes you make in your environment extends and raises your level of impact on the world around you.

When I first started this business, I had just two goals I wanted to accomplish while launching this idea with the public. The first that I didn't care about the hours or the mess. I cared about the person and the outcome. I only charged $100 per session to have enough money for gas, dinner, and a good review from working. I knew that putting this into focus would allow me room to create, make mistakes, learn, and make an impact with those that I worked with. It's always been about the people. We don't judge the mess. We work to connect with the person.

I've also trained my staff to put people over profits. If one of our organizers has a consultation with a client that has a view or mindset that doesn't alight with our core goals, we will direct them elsewhere. I've also found that when a client has worked with several different organizers and expresses dissatisfaction with each experience, they will not be happy with what I have to offer, either.

We're trying to create a relationship with the person we're spending our time with as well as make a dramatic impact in their environment. The client needs to be ready and open to have a trustful interaction with their organizer. If you remain open to the process, the organizer will have an opportunity to build trust and create some magic.

The Request

"The three c's in life: choice, chance, change. You must make the choice to take the chance if you want anything in your life to change."
—Unknown

Often, people have the misconception that organizing is simply about decluttering, arranging, and storage. But the requests we receive on a daily basis prove that making the commitment to getting organized is like hitting the reset button on life. When we first meet someone, it's like speed dating a complete stranger. In the first thirty minutes of meeting I get a full, unedited life story of what is working and what desperately needs help.

Our first meeting is an emotionally vulnerable experience for both of us. At times, I'm the only outside contact my clients feel comfortable enough with, to open up about how their clutter impacts their lives. That moment of vulnerability is sacred and personal.

Can you see a bit of yourself in these honest requests for help?

"I was mugged last year. I have since gone into deep depression and have no energy. I have lost my self-esteem and now it is really starting to affect my son. Can your team please help me find my way through the clutter?"

"We just moved my mom into an assisted living facility and need someone to spend a few hours helping her finish unpacking and organizing her things so it feels like home."

"I recently took on two foster children. Prior to this, I had no children. As always, kids come with stuff, and being foster kids, they come with lots of paperwork. The first six months I focused on surviving. Now, I want to focus on providing a safe and healing environment for all of us."

When someone calls us to organize for them, they are no longer toying with the idea of getting organized. They have finally committed to making a big change in their lives.

"I think in our current culture, women are still conditioned to think that they're supposed to be the ones managing the home and being good at it. But I have personally found in my life that hiring someone who's *way* better at organizing than I am and who's objective is making hard decisions easier, frees me up to do the things *I'm* really good at. Sometimes, the best thing you can do is release it to an expert. It's an incredible thing to be decluttered because of the freedom that comes along with it. Freedom is one of the most important values that we can have as a human being because freedom gives you options and opportunities."

—Jessica Eaves Matthews,
America's advocate for Women in Business

Consultation Questions

If the Google Maps app has been kind enough to locate your home with ease, our organizers will arrive at your home for a complimentary in-home consultation. The purpose of the consultation is to determine:

- Set goals, budgets, and timelines.
- Your organizing style, and if your preferences are different from those you live with.
- Your expectations for the organizing sessions.
- How easy it is for you to make quick decisions.
- How much are you willing to part with to make an impact.
- Your esthetic preference for organizing supplies.
- Whether you want to work with your organizer or have the work done for you.
- Whether everyone in the household is ready to have an organizer in their home.
- Whether the project will make an impact and is a good fit for everyone involved.
- Whether you have worked with an organizer before and what your experience was like.

"One of the best pieces of advice I got along my journey is fail fast. If you are doing something that's not working, don't keep doing it. Let it go. If you have something in your mind, like this is how it has to be, and it's just not clicking, either with your clients or your systems perspective, just do it differently. And that has been such a huge help, because you envision things and think they are going to go a certain way, and then they don't. And so, it's ok to let that ego go. You're not going to do things that way.

You are going to change course, and changing the course can lead you to your ultimate success."

—Lisabet De Vos Maczulajtys, Lash Factory

The Home Tour

When we arrive at a home for the first time, we look for a few indicators to predetermine what level of disorganization the client may be at, starting with the driveway.
Is these garbage or rubbish in the driveway?
Are the windows covered with sheets/blankets/broken shades?
If the porch area clean of debris?
Believe it or not, this all matters. It's true what they say about curb appeal. A first impression starts at the driveway. From there, we start assessing the state of the home and the person making the request for help. Although the client may have only a specific area in their home they would like to organize, oftentimes when the client starts there, we will have extra time to do further organizing around the home. This is why we like to conduct a full home tour. After our tour, it's not uncommon for me to start in an area that the client may not have registered as a priority starting point. Each area affects the next. An organizer has an objective eye for what will make the greatest impact in the home.

Goals and Managing Expectations

The next step is understanding your desire for the space. What do you want your space to look like? You may have a guest bedroom that's more of a storage space, or an entire closet or room that has no specific purpose other than to house random items thrown into it when guests come over. It's important for you to take some time and get clear on what you want from your space.

Once you have a clear goal in mind, the next step is mapping it out in a way that's realistic to achieve within a given time frame and budget.

Levels of Organizing

This is where we deep dive into your sense of organizing and style. Isn't it funny how everyone's sense of "clean" tends to be dramatically different?

Think about it. If you were to ask a messy teen to clean their room, what would that look like? Your definition of clean and organized may be very different than someone else's. The key to being happy with the outcome of an organized space is understanding where you are now and where you want to be.

I ask two questions to my clients:

On a scale from (1 to Martha Stewart) where are you currently? On a scale from (1 to Martha Stewart) where do you want to be?

If you're striving for Pinterest perfection, there's nothing wrong with that. I often tend to operate at that level of thinking. It's just important to take a step back to set the right foundation and remind ourselves that it takes time and money to be Martha.

Looking at where you are now, in your current cluttered space, what level of organizing do you want to get to and how much time and money can you commit to making this a reality?

Plan

After the home tour is completed and we understand your objectives, your organizer will work on a plan to tackle your clutter using the Impact Organizing Method. While many clients believe that organizing products will solve their problem, we look at the following.

- How quickly can the client make decisions?
- Is the requested space the most impactful to organize first?
- Will downsizing using products the client already possesses be impactful?
- Is there a better furniture/storage plan that can be used more efficiently in the space?

Taking the Next Steps

If you have an understanding about what it takes to create an organized life and are ready to DIY, this next chapter is for you. I will walk you through my step-by-step method of how to transform any physical space in a single day. Your time is valuable, so why not make an impact?

"I think the first step is to really think about what's important to you. Time is something that we can't get back, and so finding out how to maximize the limited amount of time that we do have. And with that, where that extra time should be placed."

—Lara Olsha, The Sweet Spot

Organizing Essentials

- A working vacuum cleaner

It's an item in our home that's easy to overlook, but it's fundamental in keeping a tidy home. Make sure your vacuum is working efficiently and is easy for you to use. If not, consider replacing your old vacuum for a more convenient option. If you are in a constant battle with your vacuum, it will block you from making real progress.

- A broom and dustpan

Often, things get left behind because they're hard to reach, or we don't have the basics needed to quickly address it. Having a good broom and dustpan handy makes for quick, clean pickup.

- A Magic Eraser

How did we ever function without them? This product is really magic and works on nearly every surface. I like to use these in the bathroom area and to remove scuffs, permanent maker, and other stubborn substances.

- Glass Cleaner

A clean glass surface can easily transform a space. If you have sticky handprints from little fingers or maybe a dog that loves to press his nose to the glass, having a clean view is essential.

- Basic Tool Set

I can fix almost anything with my Ikea tool kit!

- Zip Ties

These are also a quick fix for nearly everything around the home or office. They're great for bundling and hiding wires.

- Garbage Bags

It's essential to have good, strong, black/white garbage bags. I like to use black bags for garbage and white for donation items. This will help you stay organized and easily identify the two categories while organizing.

- Ziplock Bags

These products are great to have in varying sizes. Before you purchase containment items, I prefer to categories these items with Ziploc bags.

- Masking Tape

This are great for making quick labels on bins.

- Sticky Notes

Sticky note everything! I don't mean that literally, but using sticky notes strategically will help you categorize your large piles when organizing. Sticky notes also help others find where things are. They're great for temporally organizing piles of paperwork before you create your final organization system.

- Sharpies

I prefer the thicker sharpies for labeling my sticky notes.

- Lighter

I've seen more saved candles collecting dust than being burned and enjoyed. There's always a reason to celebrate, so let's light those candles and enjoy the moment we're creating.

- Picture Hooks

If you have more artwork and frames on your floor than on your walls, now is a good time to pick a spot and stick a nail in it.

Maintenance is Easier

It's so much easier to maintain an established system. The foundation of your system is the starting point for everything else. When you reach the baseline of what you want each area in your home to look like, maintenance is the only thing required. However, if you don't build the correct foundational systems, you'll keep running on the hamster wheel of never getting organized at all.

When you have a system in your home that works for your organizing style, it makes upkeep easy for you and others. Maintenance of your space should happen daily, monthly, and seasonally. The everyday practice of maintaining organized spaces should only take you five to ten minutes per room. When you're on top of your daily tidying, you can advance to adding a monthly purge. Cycle out things that are not used or loved on a monthly basis. Get them out of your home.

Once you've implemented these two habits, create the habit of cycling your monthly and now your seasonal items. This includes seasonal clothes, decor, gifts you've been hoarding all year that you've been meaning to give to people. (Hey—do that now!) The seasonal sweep is awesome because you get a look at the items you loved and used last season and the items you neglected. You also have the chance to pull out the new season's items and make a conscious choice about what you now love. If you don't love it or don't use it, toss it!

Music Motivates

Before you do anything, make sure you have good lighting, open any windows, and get a good flow to the room or space you're working in. Above all, turn on music! Not just any music. Music that will lift your spirits and get you in the mood for organizing. Some of my clients prefer meditation music to bring calm to the space. Others will turn on some gangster rap and whip their hair into a high bun to get it done. Whatever gets you focused. Dive into it.

Q&A with The Organizing Expert

To possess anything requires attention and maintenance. Whether you have a relationship, have a car, or own a home, everything requires effort. What are you putting your effort into? Simply acquiring things and never giving them the proper attention can lead to heartache. Whether it's a relationship or maintaining your possessions, if you don't give things the attention they need, they will end up hurting you. Every little thing adds up. If you're not grateful for what you have, you will only be met with chaos when you get more than you can handle.

Clutter isn't just the physical stuff. It could be emotional, spiritual, relationships, finances—anything. Clutter can take over many parts of our lives. It's time to be the boss and get every area of your life working to support you when you need it most. Work with what you have, simplify, then contain and fine tune your organization systems. Don't rush to buying something to fix your clutter problem. Often, when you downsize and utilize what you already have, you don't need to purchase anything.

That is the beauty of working with what you have first.

As you lean into living with less and cutting the clutter from your life, tackle your spaces one at a time. When you get one area done, you'll feel inspired and will be motivated to conquer another.

This is how you make an impact.

I've compiled a list of questions I've been asked over the years that you may have been asking yourself. What I've found most fascinating is that we all have more in common that you may think. No matter what your background, status, or religious beliefs, our homes reflect the lives we lead. Clutter is something we all have in common.

The most common question I get asked is whether or not someone's space is the worst space I've ever seen. I can say with confidence there's nothing I haven't seen. Not much scares me anymore. I've happened upon everything from dead animals to outrageous sex toys (and rooms). Whatever you have really won't surprise me.

Answers to Your Biggest Clutter Questions

Q) How do you know what to do with my stuff?

A) Impact organizing is a method that works. Just because an item is in your home doesn't mean it's unique. It may have specific requirements for management or storage, but the approach is the same. Whether you have an in-home yarn business or a private medical practice, the process for cutting the clutter and creating an impactful experience is the same.

Q) Do you just throw everything away?
A) Although at times I would like to just light a match or throw it away, that is never an option. You don't need to throw everything away and start over, either. You simply need to uncover what's important and discard what isn't. If you find it difficult to detach from a certain item, extend the experience by offering that item to someone else.

Q) What's the difference between a Professional Organizer and an Organizing Expert?
A) A professional organizer has typically purchased a membership through the National Association of Professional Organizers (NAPO) and will work alone to coach you. He or she may also help organize with a team in a specific niche like hoarding, ADD, senior downsizing, etc.

An Organizing Expert is trained with the primary goal to create a visual change and transformational experience using the Impact Organizing Method. No matter what the physical space, the intention is to give the client the biggest visual impact in the shortest amount of time.

Q) How do I organize my "sexy box?" (Everyone has one. Or many.)
A) It's nothing to be ashamed or embarrassed of. What is embarrassing is inviting an expert to come organize your bedroom only to find your used vibrator just lying on the floor collecting dog hair. Having a healthy and sanitary way to store and organize your sexual items is important. All you need to do is keep your items contained in a discrete, clean location. If you're in the adult industry or into something more explicit, I'm not the expert for your job.

Q) How should I organize photos?
Please, please, please, don't shove them away! Downsizing your physical photos is important. Writing who and where the photo took place is important. It's essential to keep them in a place you can easily access on a rainy day. They're memories to reflect on.

You can get real Martha Stewart with it and make scrapbooks or albums, but it's not necessary. Just get them where you can look at them. If you have a ton of digital photos, print them! We can get overloaded with the accessibility of our smart phone to take photos. It's a wonderful thing to go through your phone and create albums. Keeping your digital photos on a backup hard drive or uploading them to the cloud is not a bad idea, either. Just make sure to look at them and store them properly to prevent any damage.

Q) What do I do with all my VHS tapes?
A) I know Costco has an awesome option for converting your VHS into DVD's. My dear friend Jenell Thompson, owner and operator of CorporateCondo.net, hired someone off Craigslist to convert her home videos for her parent's anniversary party. She was able to stream all these videos for everyone to watch right off a hard drive. It's all about preserving and creating a memory.

Q) How should I organize my books/magazines?
A) Tony Robbins once said, "Wealthy people have a large library and poor people have big TV's." While I believe that to be true, I also think that hoarding a bunch of books and magazines isn't essential for your image.

Often, our ego tells us that a large collection of books means that we're smart. No—it just means that you have a lot of books. I've seen people shuffle so many boxes of books they will never read and only get to move from place to place collecting dust. I've moved plenty in my lifetime, and I can tell you how heavy they are! Keep the books that you love and the ones you'll reference. Everything else is just clutter.

You may think, "But I love all my books!" Then go on with your bad self and keep them. If you must keep them, then you must honor and maintain them. Magazines have a way of piling up and making you feel guilty for not reading them. Drop the guilt—it's just paper.

Magazines are designed by a team of experts for the only purpose of your consumption. Keep a small stack in downtime spots like the bathroom or outside on a covered deck. My ultimate favorite is using my magazines as a laptop stand, so when I need a quick break, I simply just pull one and done! That way, when you have that magical moment for light reading, your magazines will be at your fingertips. Done worry, by the time you get around to reading that US Weekly, Taylor Swift will already be dating someone else.

Q) How can I get caught up on paperwork?
A) Put it all in one pile. One pile. Then, tackle each piece one at a time. You can design many ways to organize the paperwork chaos, but to get it all under control in the shortest amount of time, separate your papers into the following categories.

- To file
- To shred
- To recycle
- Projects

Once you've recycled and shredded, you're down to filing and projects. You can create a simplified file system with like categories and keep your projects in one "To-Do" file. Every time a piece of paper hits your desk make the decision to file, toss, or make time to complete the project. That is all it takes to keep up with your office system.

Q) How do I stay organized?
A) Every day, declutter an area of your life. Staying organized is a practiced habit. To maintain living with less, always look for places to audit your life.

Q) How do I keep my mail from piling up?
A) Mail always has a way of getting out of control if we don't actively control it. As soon as mail enters your home or office, you need to make the decision to recycle or shred the items you don't need, then keep the rest in their designated zones. You can also check out services to help opt out of junk mail and catalogs. Paper Karma is a great option.

Q) How do I manage to get all my errands done?
A) Batching your errands. I encourage my clients to get a large bag and set it by the door closest to your car. When the bag is full, take it to the car and batch your errands together. Put aside one day for running around. Batching your outside tasks like "returns" or "to office" on a specific day cuts back on constantly running around. Labeled bags, even paper ones, are a great way to start batching your errands. It doesn't have to be complicated. It just has to work.

Q) How do I simplify my beauty routine?
A) Imagine you're in a hurry and you only have a few minutes to get ready. What do you cut? Observe the products you cut from your routine and ask yourself if you can cut that from your life. Usually, we own more products than we ever actually use. Sticking with the basics can save you from overstocking beauty products and creating chaos on your countertop. If limiting products doesn't work for you, at least make sure to go through and toss old products. We can spend so much money

on makeup and hair product that we keep them long past their expiration. Ew.

Q) Help! I have too many apps!
A) Most everyone these days has a smartphone. Do you ever get a message that your phone is almost out of storage? That's a polite way of saying that you're a digital hoarder. Time to move all the unused apps to a page on your phone that you don't use often and group your most frequently used apps on your main screen. If you don't use an app within thirty days, delete it from your phone and save storage space. Once a week, give your photos a quick glance and delete any unnecessary screenshots or pictures that you wouldn't want to keep for a lifetime.

4 | One-Day Transformation

In the beginning of my career I was only organizing parts of the problem but not treating the whole home lifestyle to bring about a solution. I started playing a game with myself: Every time the client would come back into the room, I would change the environment in such a way as to make a visual difference.

My goal was to hear the client say, "WOW, how did you do that?!" every time they came back to check on the progress of their space. Each time, my assistant would keep score on how many times my client would say "WOW" throughout the day. I knew I was onto something.

The intention for my method was simple: provide my clients with a one-day transformation.

Who wants to take forever to get organized, anyway? That was a common complaint with many of my clients who had sought organizing help elsewhere. I know many of my colleagues were well-intentioned organizers. However, I had seen an increase in the number of professionals who were charging a hefty hourly rate and were more interested in the payout rather than producing an overall transformation of the space.

Fluffy organizing, as I sweetly dubbed it, is when an individual gives themselves the title "professional organizer" simply because they come armed with a label maker. A clear bin of socks doesn't require a label. Call me crazy, but I don't think you need a label for everything.

Isn't it rather time-consuming to spend all your time making sticky labels?

My single objective was to visually transform a person's space. To make my mark, and make it known that an expert had done some damage for the better. I wanted each of my clients to have an experience. This is my impact on the world through each and every home I enter. I want it to be better and lighter than when I arrived.

There are few things in life that are as liberating and instantly gratifying as getting organized and decluttering your space. Let me break it down for you into some simple action steps. I encourage you to take this method step-by-step and choose one area of your home to focus on, like the entryway to your home. Set an alarm on your phone for sixty minutes of interrupted organizing. In the words of one of my favorite hit songs by Montell Jordan, "This is how we do it!"

Step 1: Make a plan and take a photo

Look at your room and take a picture from the doorway. Now look at the photo and ask yourself what would make the biggest visual impact. Give yourself time to write down a plan of action.

Step 2: Floor space

Often, my clients don't know where to start. I always, always, always start with the floor. Why the floor? Because I'm an accomplishment junkie and I get instant gratification when one thing is checked off my to-do list. By starting with the floor, it's easy to mark this zone as one-and-done. Even if you put everything that is on the floor onto a surface space, you've completed the task of getting everything off the floor. Now, as you're going along cleaning your floor space, please make sure to get rid of any obvious garbage and recycling as well. I mean, really get rid of it. Get it out of your house altogether. That floor should be free and clear!

Step 3: Set a Time Limit

The reason we set a time limit is so that no moment is wasted. If you can dedicate a consistent amount of time to this project, you're more likely to keep at it and stay focused. Many people start with the intention of organizing and don't give themselves a proper timeline for accomplishing it. When I'm working with clients, I look at a space and dissect each step with a time limit. For each of the steps, give yourself an estimated time and set a timer on your phone to complete each step. For example, in Step 2, you will be focusing on the floor space. How much time do you think it will take to clear the floor? Make sure to break this down and hold yourself accountable by setting a timer. Now go, baby. Go!

Step 4: Clear it out

Clear out any obvious garbage and recycle and remove it from your home. Don't just tag these items and stack them in a pile. Make a bag for garbage and a bag for recycling. Keep these two bags handy as you begin working on the surface space in the room where you're currently working.

Step 5: Categorize

Now it's time to tackle the surface. Your floor zone should be free and clear at this point. Congratulations! If your floor is clear, you've just completed one zone of the Impact Organizing Method. Here in Step 5, focus on making large single categories of items. All paperwork, if possible, should go into one pile labeled "paperwork." As you move through the room, collect like items and give them a large category name. You want to gain a quick sense of accomplishment, so start with a pile that doesn't belong in the current space and relocate it to where it belongs. For example, if you have a bunch of clothes in your office, that would be an easy pile to gather and relocate.

Step 6: Downsize

Now it's time to downsize your large category piles. The easiest decisions to make are the obvious ones. Not sure what clothes to get rid of first? Start with your crusty underwear that you need to get rid of.
Wow. That was gross.

Seriously, start with something obvious that you can part with. Once you've done this, the decision-making process has already started in your brain. Making harder decisions will become crystal clear. Organize each pile of like items to completion, one pile at a time. Leave the paperwork for last. Paperwork can be tedious and is the most time-consuming to organize.

Step 7: Contain and label

This is where you can get all Martha Stewart. It's only at this step that I suggest possibly purchasing any items that would better contain the space or items in it. Here's where you evaluate your storage solutions. Everything you have in your room should be something useful that falls under one of your large categories. Keep and contain only what matters. If you ask yourself what really matters to you, it will be easier to eliminate useless items. If an item doesn't matter, there's no reason to keep it.

It's equally as important to contain your items in a way that makes them easy to find. Put items that fall into large categories into large bins. That way, you won't have to worry about what the inside contents look like, and you have a centralized location for all the items in that category. If the bin starts overflowing, you know it's time to purge!

Step 8: Placement

Now that you've gone through your items and everything you wish to keep is contained in a large category or bin, it's time to find it a "home." When organizing a kitchen, for example, I always place dishes in the cupboard closest to where I'm unloading the dishwasher. You want every item placed efficiently in terms of your daily life. You wouldn't want to unload the dishwasher frequently and have to run around the kitchen putting away frequently used items. Thinking of your morning routine, what items do you use all the time that are stored inefficiently? I call these areas our "prime real estate" spaces. Everything you use often should be right at eye level or within easy reach.

Step 9: Rearrange

Never forget the power of rearranging your furniture! This step can transform your space dramatically, either by eliminating furniture or adding furniture to the space you already own. Rearranging gives new life to the space. Think of how you could rearrange your bedroom for a better flow. When I was young, my mom would take advantage of the time she had while I was away from school and rearrange my room without telling me. I loved it! I always thought it looked cool and different. Here, the theory worked for me. I just needed to see everything I loved in a different way. Moving rooms was not an option but rearranging everything in it was!

Step 10: Get it out

If you want real transformation, you've got to remove clutter from your environment. Moving the "donate" bag to the garage to eventually end up in the car is not part of making an impact. Complete the clutter cycle. My rule of thumb for decluttering is to have a minimum of three garbage bags full of items to donate. They then go straight into the trunk of my car, ready to drop off at my local charity. It's possible to transform your space without removing items, but to fully understand the power in this method, make a conscious effort to fill your trunk each and every time.

Step 11: Progress, not perfection

What matters is progress—not perfection. Particularly with larger projects, it's good to have documentation that supports you in pursuing a long-term goal. ALWAYS take a before and after photo of any project. That way, you can remind yourself of the progress you've already made. It's easy to get discouraged if you don't have a reference of how far you've come. When organizing, things have to get messier before they can get better. Having a before and after photo is like having a cheerleader in your pocket. Who wouldn't want that? Before you start any project, take a photo. Always celebrate with an after photo and a job well done.

Isn't this a lot?

Change takes time. Often, change is uncomfortable. When we're feeling overwhelmed with clutter in our physical space, it's hard to know where to start. Are you prone to procrastination? When you see a big mess that needs attention, would you rather do anything else to avoid dealing with it?

If you're feeling overwhelmed, your self-talk may go something like this:

- "Sweet. Another mess to pick up."
- "Maybe I should just move it somewhere else. I don't know where, but somewhere."
- "I'll just do it tomorrow."
- "Wait, I've got a free hour. I'll just run out and go get my nails done.
- This mess will be here tomorrow...

It's crazy how our self-talk can eat up valuable time and whisk us to procrastination destination. In the time that it takes to think about all of that junk, I could have already tidied up and moved onto making a memory doing something more important. Typically, we feel this way because every project and every room can seem overwhelming when left unattended for long periods of time.

If you're feeling overwhelmed, you need some little wins.

You've got to structure your time so that it has a beginning and an end. The sense of drowning means that it's a fight. We want to ease this sense of discomfort by picking a small, manageable task to complete. If you feel good after your first project, feel free to move on, but give yourself a time limit. Just like book writing, if I set a structure of five-minute increments I get so much done. If I give myself the whole day and don't set my timer, life has a way of creeping in and taking over my time.

I've outlined a few quick thirty-minute projects. These tend to be common problem areas for most of us in our homes. Set a timer on your phone for thirty minutes and tackle one small project. Again, we only want to focus on creating "little wins."

Having accomplished a task will positively reinforce our ability to move on to bigger and better projects.

Front Door/Entryway

I urge my clients to remove themselves from their home. Go on a short walk and return home with a fresh perspective. Your entryway is a great place to start. The routine is familiar to you, and in order to see it in a different light, you need a fresh perspective. Ask yourself what you can eliminate from the space.

Your entryway tends to be a catchall for everything and everyone in the house. Now that you're in this space with fresh eyes, grab a piece of paper, a pen, and a timer. Before setting your timer, make a list of everything you see that bothers you. Then, when you've identified your problem areas, set your timer to thirty minutes and work your list from top to bottom.

Start by removing any trash, breaking down boxes, and getting rid of recycling. Relocate any items that don't belong, then take an audit of what needs to stay. Eliminate things that are not quick "grab-and-go" items. When you enter your home, it should comfort you and have a basic structure for frequently used items.

This is a great project to start on. Assess jackets and seasonal items that can be downsized.

Refrigerator

When was the last time you wiped out all the shelves and bins in your refrigerator? I bet you it's been a hot minute. This is a great thirty-minute project. Start with trash bag in hand and get rid of anything that's old, expired, or growing a new ecosystem. Then, take all the items out and place all the contents on one, clean surface space in the kitchen. Wipe out the entire refrigerator and place a new deodorizer in the back to keep your items nice and fresh. This is also a great time to check for any leaks.

Now that you've audited and cleaned your refrigerator, you'll want to put items back in an organized way that makes sense for you and your home. Placing "grab-and-go" items in your prime real estate spots is important. Don't forget to designate an easy-to-reach drawer or shelf for your kids' snacks. Frequently used items should always be placed front and center. I also like to have a shelf dedicated to leftovers as well as a space for prepped ingredients.

Car

Whether you're a busy parent on the go or rushing from job to home, the car can be an overwhelming catchall area. It's time to address those smashed goldfish crackers in the backseat or the late-night Taco Bell smells coming from the passenger seat.

I always ask myself, If Oprah was stranded on the side of the road, would I be ready to rescue her? You never know who may get in your car, whether it's your boss who needs a last-minute lift or a friend trapped in the rain. Believe it or not, the organization of your car is a huge first impression of who you are and how you run your life.

Every time you stop for gas, empty all the trash from your car. This is a great habit to adapt. Keep frequently used items close at hand and have organizers in your car so that every item has a specific home. Since items are often coming and going, it's great to have a bin system in place in the trunk of your car. Always be sure to have an emergency pack prepared and properly stored.

Pets: Room to Roam

If you have pets, you know the nature of animals who freely give you love and excitement every time they see you. All you have to do is walk in the room! What a gift pets are to our lives. We humans don't always show love as easily and freely as our little soul-keepers, and we owe it to them to keep a tidy home.

Our pets see life from only a few feet off the ground. If your floor space is cluttered, they get very confused.

Animals need lots of clear space, to roam, play, and sleep. Sure, you may see that they're entertained playing with that lost bottle cap for hours, but that doesn't justify you being too lazy to pick it up.

Let's be clear: You owe it to them to keep the space tidy and free of garbage. Your floor space is where they spend their entire existence. It's common for animals, specifically cats, to get territorial or confused by clutter and want to urinate on items.

When I first started working with hoarders, I would see cats blamed for defecating everywhere. The truth is, when cats feel confined, they will go anywhere they think there is space. Can we all agree that there's nothing worse than cat urine? Yes, some animals can do this out of spite, but for many animals, they feel ashamed when they have an accident on the floor.

It's essential to tackle the floor space in each room in your house. Open space is a must if you own large, indoor dogs. Look at ways you can create more space and downsize your furniture. While you're down there, clean that floor! In ten years of organizing, I've never seen anyone over vacuum. You may have a few dust-bunnies, unknown hairballs, or other things that may have already taken on a life of their own.

Don't be embarrassed if you find that your pet had an accident in the corner of the living room months ago. Just clean it up. You can always just clean it up. It doesn't matter if you're rich or poor, have a big house or a small house—I can confidently say social status has nothing to do with how you keep your home.

Once you've cleared your floor spaces, look at where and how you're storing your pet's food and accessories.

Toys should be in one central area for quick cleanup. I like to keep dog toys in a bin by my front door. That way, when I find them scattered around the house, cleanup is super easy. Also, be sure to audit dog treats for expiration. Keep treats in a centralized location as well as collars, poop bags, clothes, and leashes. Your pets' stuff should have a designated spot in your home for a quick tidy. I prefer to keep my treats near my leash. That way, my dogs learn to come quickly to get leashed and are immediately rewarded for listening.

Remember to keep your pets' dry food in a sealed storage container. You know who also likes the smell of pet food in your pantry? Rodents and pests! Keep these critters detoured by keeping your food stored in an airtight container.

When deciding what items to keep and what items to part with, having some careful self-talk is important. I've prepared a list of ten questions to ask yourself as you begin to declutter every room in your house.

Still stumped?

Here are ten questions to help you declutter every room in your home.

- Do I need this?
- Does this make me feel happy?
- Have I used this within the past year?
- If I were out shopping, would I buy this?
- Am I holding onto this for sentimental value?
- Is this something I use regularly?
- Do I feel obligated to keep this?
- Am I saving this "just in case" I need it in the future?
- Is this worth the time and effort to keep, store, and maintain?
- Could I use this space for something else by letting this go?

Three Common Areas to Save for Later

Since we are looking to create a lasting impact, we want to start off with projects that create an instant feeling of gratification. Too often I'm hired, to help clients who can't see past their own clutter. For some, they're operating from that "fight or flight mode" and find themselves trapped thinking they have to tackle the hardest issue first. In my experience, this isn't going to give you the biggest impact.

Here are three common areas of clutter that I recommend tackling after you've finished working through the Impact Organizing Method on the overall space. These problem areas can rob you of your time and sanity if you try to tackle them first.

Laundry

It's important to establish a laundry system that works for your family. Each home is slightly different, but the same sock-monster seems to live in every home I've visited. While you may feel compelled to make laundry your first priority in order to slay the elusive, sock-stealing-monster, I urge you to wait. Yes, having separate bins either by category or person is important, but you can easily get lost doing laundry for hours. Once you've worked the method on a larger skill (i.e., have organized the whole laundry room), then you can get to the laundry. Trust me. It will still be there waiting for you.

Paperwork

Paperwork takes the longest of any category to organize. Adopt these mantras.

- I will downsize my paperwork.
- I will identify what I need to keep and what I can toss/shred using the Paper Retention Guide. *Found on OrganizingExperts.com*
- I will wait and tackle my paper clutter once I've made an impact on my overall space.

Someone Else's Clutter

I'm organized, but may partner / kid / sister / brother / mother / aunt / uncle / grandparent (fill in the blank) is not!
Really?
There may be truth to this statement, but let's take a look at your organized lifestyle. Make sure that your part of the world is conquered before you start exploring someone else's. Children tend to model after their parents. Partners tend to do their own thing until they understand how important it is to us

to maintain an organized home. It's up to you and you alone to set that standard.

You can only control yourself, and it's so much more fulfilling when you accomplish your own goals rather than someone else's.

Items that Require Someone Else's Approval

Pick areas where you and you alone can make quick decisions. If everything is someone else's decision, they need to be the one doing the work. Determine who has the okay to make the final decision and make them thoughtfully and swiftly. It's often a popular misconception that when I arrive at someone's home to organize, I'll be "getting rid of everything." My job as an Organizing Expert is to organize your environment in a way that's easiest for you to make impactful decisions. Determining who will make the executive decisions on which items stay and go is essential.

Garage (In the Off-Season)

I'm not sure what it is, but the moment the weather changes for the worst is the same moment people want to tackle the garage. It's human nature, I suppose. It's best to prep for the season ahead so that when it starts snowing outside, you can park your car in the garage. On a nice, sunny day, pull everything out, work the method, and tackle the garage. Not during the off-season when it's freezing, raining, snowing, dark, and cold. (Your hired organizers will thank you in advance.)

Keepsakes

Choosing to dive into your most emotional belongings first is a surefire way to burn out quickly and lose momentum. Again, wait on these items and give them the appropriate time and space to make rational decisions rather than emotional ones. If you've worked the method and are ready to tackle this project, employ an outside perspective—someone who doesn't have an emotional interest and can align your goals to your current reality. What may have served as an emotional interest may be different at this stage in your life. Downsizing your keepsake items can be very emotionally charged, and I recommend giving those items the time and respect they need to make thoughtful decisions.

Remember that this is your space, you own your domain. We want to gain as much momentum as we can by focusing on the overall most impactful tasks first, then the smaller problem areas after. You've worked hard to have the space you're in right now. Do you remember when you used to dream for things to be better?
Then they were, and somewhere along the way, we got derailed.

Our house feels a bit tragic at times, and the never-ending to-fix list masks the comfort of being home.

It's okay. It happens to all of us. Everything living thing and every one of us need a little room to just keep breathing.

Part of the reason why we hold on to some things so tightly is because we fear that something so great won't happen twice. But the magic is in the leap. Have faith that when you let go, something bigger and better is just around the corner.

Letting Go

My grandparents live on a modest eleven-and-a-half acres in a small, A-framed home in the Pacific Northwest. My Papa moved from the city in 1973 with a dream. He packed up his wife, trailer, and a few pigs. At the time, my Papa didn't have much money, but he did have hustle in his heart. He sold the pigs who lived under his trailer, and little by little, he built the home that my grandmother lives in today.

When my Papa passed away, I was hit instantly with so many emotions and responsibilities to process. I was sad because I no longer had the patriarch of my family, someone above me who could always chuckle about my troubles. I felt anger for all the things he'd left undone. I felt overwhelmed and confused over the amount of clutter, garbage, and junk that he took such great pride in.

His belongings were everything to him. He grew up without a family and never owned anything of worth until making his life at the farm. He felt his self-worth was tied to all he had acquired. He didn't seek to own *quality* possessions—quantity to him represented success. I was left with a lot of *"could be great items if fixed, but good luck finding parts because it's made in China"* items.

Since his passing, I've cleaned over 10,000 tons of garbage and clutter. I knew my Papa's worth was never contained in his belongings, but in all the lessons, laughter and memories I will have for a lifetime. There are a few trinkets left behind of no real monetary value, but these keepsakes bring me the most joy in his absence.

Giving and Re-gifting

Do you feel guilty for not using a gift you received? How do you feel about re-gifting? What gifts have you gotten that are just sitting around making you feel guilty? Don't be afraid to part with gifts you've received. I give you permission to get rid of it!

The best advice I've ever listened to on the energy of a gift came from my queen, Oprah Winfrey. I heard her beautifully explain in an interview that the energy is in the giving of the gift, not in the gift itself. We tend to hold onto the moment long after it's gone. No one wants you to feel guilty for not liking a gift you were given.

The best thing to do is free yourself of the guilt and re-gift the item to someone else. Transfer the good energy and pass it along.

Moments are experiences that are only kept in our memory.

Moments cannot be placed into things. Giving any physical item so much emotional energy could end in much more heartache. Our physical world is temporary and can be lost, stolen, or broken.

Gifting to Those in Need

Your clutter can actually serve your community. One of our founding ideas was to open the conversation around Seattle's homelessness epidemic with Care Kits.

Care Kits are simply little bags you can put behind the passenger seat of your car to hand out the window to those who are homeless and asking for help. Our Care Kits are filled with "once loved items" from clients—snacks, handwarmers, travel toiletries, etc. While you may not be comfortable giving money, a Care Kit will put once-loved items into the hands of those who need them most.

A Man Named Russ

A homeless man named Russ, who wanders my neighborhood block in Belltown patiently watching life from his wheelchair. One day, I decided that since he and I both share the same block, I should know my neighbors better. Instead of walking pass with my head down, I stopped and asked him if he needed anything. He said he would like a cigarette.

I couldn't believe my ears! Of *all* the things you could need in this world, you want a cigarette?!

I told him I didn't have any cigarettes, then decided to introduce myself and continue the conversation. From that day forward, I vowed that I may not be able to offer him what he wants, but I can offer him recognition and compassion. Every day I see him, I stop, say hello, and ask him how his day is.

One day while helping a client who also utilizes a wheelchair, it seemed I finally had an accessory that could make a difference for Russ. I was excited to see him and give deliver some new accessories to "enhance his ride." On our next encounter, I gave him a seat cushion specifically designed for his wheelchair, then knelt beside him and attached his new cup holder strap. His eyes widened as I knelt on the street helping him. We chatted for a bit, and he told me how grateful he was that I thought of him.

Two days later, I saw Russ with no cushion and no cup holder.

At first, I felt upset that I had gone to the trouble to gift these items to him, and he didn't even want them. I was annoyed—those things could have gone to someone else more grateful to have them. The truth of it is, I had set too much of an expectation on what *I thought* was best for him. Why did I think that things made more of an impact on humanity than simple recognition?

The lesson here?

Let go of the judgement or story you've created around someone else's needs. You may have a negative opinion on how they will use the items you give. That's not what the act of giving is about. Give without expectation or understanding of the outcome.

Judgement is not the job of the giver. To give someone a gift is an extension of kindness. It's the act of giving, not the outcome. When you give, it is the receivers an invitation to their own experience.

Many people feel uncomfortable handing money to those panhandling on the street. I get it. So how can we flip the script? How can we make an impact? I think the very unnecessary things that we've been holding onto or unused could really make a difference to someone who has nothing. Be it old blankets, pillows, or those travel-sizes dental supplies you get from the dentist. All these little things can create a care kit you can keep in your car. So instead of ignoring the human soul asking for help, offer them something. If they don't want it, they will tell you. Have a conversation and offer what you can with what you have. You never know whose life you'll impact, and it takes zero effort to drive through a neighborhood that you'd typically avoid on your way to any donation site. Take a moment to create an experience of giving.

"I know it never seems like a priority, but your external world is always representative of your inner state. The more you can declutter and organize your outer state, it can literally help you create the same internally."

– Bri Seeley, Permission to Leap

5 | The Truth About Keeping Everything in Order

The truth is, keeping everything organized all the time, in my opinion, is not realistic, nor is it the goal. I know this may seem like a surprising statement from an Organizing Expert, but I believe in creating a space that's maintainable and realistic. The notion of keeping it all together is like trying to keep up with the Kardashians. It's not a realistic lifestyle for most. I believe in allowing room for life to happen.
What are your intentions for your space?

Have you ever walked into someone's house, afraid that your presence alone could be a threat to the space you're in? It doesn't feel warm and inviting.

I don't know about you, but I would rather spend my days in a home that is well lived in. This isn't to say that I don't like nice things or the maintenance it takes to preserve them. I've been blessed to see and live in both worlds, and neither is better than the other. My work as an organizer has given me the experience of living and working in the most beautiful homes you can imagine, and it all requires maintenance.

How do you achieve clarity and create a realistic framework for keeping things organized?

Try asking yourself these questions.

- What is your intention for the space?
- Is entertaining your focus?
- Do you have pets/kids/partners sharing your space?
- What do you want your home to look/feel like?
- Do you want to keep more or discard more?
- What is your lifestyle? Rushed or relaxed?
- How much time do you want to spend each day organizing?

Take some time to identify what's happening in your current space and what you want it to be. The goal here is to see what's working, what's not working, and to create a realistic framework for keeping a more organized lifestyle on a routinely basis.

Create "Drop Spots"

Is there anything worse than loss? I think so. The fear of loss is worse. When something is confirmed to be lost, at least you have closure. That frantic, uncertain feeling you get when you feel something is lost can be downright awful. Whether you've lost your car keys in the morning or lost your child in a department store, the feeling of loss can be devastating.

How many times a day does your body feel the fear of losing something? This is something to really bring awareness to. If you're in a constant state of losing things, you're also in a constant state of uncertainty and worry. Eliminating the hunt for lost items will not only dramatically free up your life but also cut out so much stress. It's so easy to lose time simply by looking for everyday essentials. Take back those lost minutes by creating consistent "drop spots" for everyday items like your car keys, dirty laundry, purse, you child's backpack, and so on.

Family Systems

When it comes to family systems, no two are the same. You need to see what currently works and assess how to make it better. I've interviewed a few incredible women to see how they implement systems that bring peace to the piles.

Fighting the Mom Guilt—A Real Client Story

Mom guilt is real, and it can be directly impacted by your organizing life.

Do you relate to this client's story?

I imagine it going I see on TV. I let you guys in, I leave, and then I come back to find it all transformed. I know that's real, but it's what I crave. That's my fantasy! I've been saying this for years. I just want to get it under control.

I just look at the enormity of the task, and it's paralyzing. I used to joke with my friends that I'd love for someone to come over and just crack the whip like my mother used to do. She would tell me to go up there and get it done—that I wasn't allowed to go anywhere until my room was clean.

It's not a matter of wanting to get organized. I do. It's just the enormity of the project that seems impossible. Or, at least, getting it to a point I can manage. It feels so enormous that the clutter is eating my life away just thinking about it.

I never feel like I have enough quality of time. I'm always multitasking, and I feel like I'm half everywhere. I'm half helping my son. I'm half cleaning the house, half making dinner... I'm just done. I'm trying to pay the bills and answer the door for the contractor at the same time. No person's brain functions well this way.

I feel guilty that I'm not doing enough—guilty that I'm not teaching my child enough and that I'm not doing enough for them. I also feel guilty that I'm not calling my parents enough. The list goes on and on...

THE TRUTH: Hopes and dreams aren't going to fix this. If I learn to detach, delegate, and live a simplified and organized life, it's going to allow me to spend more quality of time with my kids. I know that's what they really crave and what matters the most."

—Andrea C. of Seattle, WA

How do You Avoid Burnout?

No one knows how to stay more organized than a military wife. Rebekah Adams is the owner of Poppyseed Clothing, mother, and military spouse who lives and breathes functionality.

Having a kid and being a solo parent when my husband is on deployment—all while trying to run my business—you have to be on top of stuff. think that being a military spouse means you're going to be a solo parent for part of the time, whether it's training or deployment. For part of the time everything is going to rely on you. It's critical to create structure to avoid burnout.

Creating Daily Habits

If making the bed is the foundation of your daily routine, teach your children the same thing. Before you're even fully awake, you've already accomplished a huge organizing goal of putting your room together. I believe in teaching kids that nothing belongs on the floor and that every possession should have a home. This creates the habit of respect. Even if the surface spaces become temporarily cluttered, keep the floor a clutter-free zone. Simplify the process and help your child to find a home for the things living on surface areas. Just as we tuck our children into bed at night, they can also understand that belongings also need to be "tucked in" their proper places to rest.

Grouping Like Toys Together Helps Focused Playtime

It's important to organize toys in a manageable way. The first and easiest way is to minimize the volume of toys. Quality trumps quantity. Then, purchase small to medium plastic bins and make either written or picture labels. Group toys into large category items. Avoid getting lost in keeping unnecessary toys from birthday parties, McDonalds, etc. Trinkets that are merely distractions don't serve any real purpose other than to drive you crazy and leave you unsure of what to do them.

Take it from me, it's okay to donate the old McDonald's toys that have never been opened. Kids will play with garbage and items that should really be in the recycle bin. Just because they can play with those items doesn't mean they should.

Give your playroom more structure. Separate toys into categories, fun and educational. The next step is to teach your child to pull one organized bin at a time, empty the contents,

play, and then dump the toys back into bin before pulling out another project. This creates more structure to playtime.
Start playtime with a simple question.
What do you feel like playing with today?

Helping your child get specific and intentional about what they want to do helps guide them. If left to their own devices, they will likely just start pulling everything off the shelves until they find something that tickles their fancy—and leave you with the aftermath of the tornado.

It Starts at Childhood

I sat down with one of my favorite portrait photographers, Michelle Moore, to see what organizing habits are most important to her. She handles all aspects of her business, and I was curious to see how she stayed organized. Has she always been an organized person?
She shared with me a single concept that her mother had taught her when she was only five years old.

Being organized is very important to me. Many times, I've heard from clients how appreciative they are of my communication and being able to deliver images to them in a timely manner. I take great pride in these skills and strongly believe they have played a major impact in where I am in my career. I've actually always been very neat and organized ever since I was a kid. It's just part of who I am, but I do clearly remember a pivotal point in when I became really into it. When I was about five or six, I remember an epic cleaning/organizing day with my mom when we went through my entire room...and cleaned up/organized everything.

My mom said to me, 'Now, next time you go out to play with something, make sure you put one group of toys away before getting out the next one". That moment stuck with me, and I think led me to stay really organized throughout my entire childhood and into my adult life.

Manage Paper Flow Like an Adult

Typically, my adult clients are one or the other when it comes to being organized at the office or at home. Seldom are they both. When your work environment is structured and systematized, it's easy to manage the flow of paperwork and projects efficiently. The same is true for setting up a paper flow system at home. Do you have an inbox for artwork, homework, and other categories? Having a central scheduling system is also helpful, be it digital or physical, so everyone in the house can see what's on the weekly agenda. The kids' paperwork should be managed near the kitchen or the front door.

The reason you want to have an organized paper system near the door is because this is where all the traffic happens in the morning and at night. Before you leave for school, it's easy to stop grab your book bag, jacket, and paperwork from the same spot. The same is true when they come home. They can dump their backpacks and jackets on hooks, empty their school bag of paperwork to organize into categories and tasks, then empty their lunch bags before going any further into the house.

Making Organizing Fun

When it comes to children and clutter, meaningful conversations and consistency is key. If your child is emotionally attached to items, there's typically a strong story as to why they have a hard time letting go. Sometimes, parents implement cleaning or organizing as a punishment rather than a game. If you explain the process like a teacher would to her class, the process of letting go becomes exciting, especially if you include the rewarding outcome of having them gift items to another child.

Explain that it's a good thing to love your items and let them go—that their unused toys and clothes that no longer fit are going to help other children in need. For Example, make a monthly habit of taking your child and their items to your local Children's Home Society so they can actively participate in the cycle of their belongings. Then, they can understand the process of cycling life's possessions. This really helps them connect the dots visually and understand that they have an impact on the world around them. Children are so resilient and pure. I've seen this process transform families. It's a beautiful memory and a great habit to create with your children.

Setting the Foundation for Success

When should you start organizing with your child? It's a question I'm asked often, and my answer is to always start now. That's like asking when you should start brushing your kids' teeth. I don't care whether they're three months or twenty-four years old. Get in there and set some organizational groundwork!

When you think of a tornado, you typically think of a storm that causes mass chaos outdoors. For many of my clients, children have manifested into small tornados that leave a daily path of destruction in their homes.

Same goes with organization and downsizing. Before you put the pressure on your children to be organized, you should lead by example in all areas of your home. They will be looking to you for guidance and structure. They'll also tell you where you fall short in organizing your life. Leading by example doesn't mean you need to strive for perfection. I'm simply asking that you pay close attention to your personal routines. We want to pass on the gift of a tidy, loving home to our children that we can make memories in the sun rather than constantly cleaning up after the storm. My advice to parents is to find out what their kids love and what they don't.

What does your child truly love?

Why do you need to know how your child views things?

I challenge you to have the conversation with your little one and get on their level. Let them lead the conversations. You can prompt their responses by answering the following questions.

- What do you love to play with the most?
- What would you like to give to someone else to play with because you don't really love it so much anymore?
- What toys do you think are "baby toys?"
  (This last question is gold.)

The majority of little kids want to be big kids. When you talk about things being "age appropriate," you might be shocked at what they think is too "baby" for them. I should also caution that you may struggle with this last question. You may have just bought a forty-dollar toy that your little one tires of two seconds after getting it. That reality can crush you on a mental and financial level. Just because they don't love that item anymore doesn't mean that you can't find it a home where someone else may love it.

Hopefully, you can resell the item on Craigslist or another resell marketplace. Who doesn't want some extra cash?

How to Stop the Toy Tornado

Step 1: Let your child know they will be getting their very own donation bin in their room.

Step 2: Give them a bit of control within their own space. If they put on clothing they don't like or feel uncomfortable in, allow them a space to organize once-loved-items to potentially donate. They can also put in toys that they think is "too baby" or that they no longer play with. Ultimately, you have the last say in what leaves the home but having them practice cycling out items is a great foundation step.

Step 3: Now it's a game. As soon as they fill their bin, let them know you will take a special trip to your local charity to see your once-loved items get a new home in the community. Better yet, find a *little friend* that they can "gift" these items to. Have fun with it and take the opportunity to create an experience. Lifestyle is best taught through experiences.

Attachment Disorder

What becomes the most shocking is the parent's emotional attachment to their children's belongings. In some cases, it's the parents that aren't ready to face the reality of their children growing out of that tiny adorable, Oshkosh overalls or their once-beloved Shopkins. Parents' don't be the hindrance in the downsizing process!

> "I have three kids, and we've learned to gather as much as we can, put it in the laundry room, and once it is all clean, fold and organize by the person. Each child has a role, and the main call to action is to keep it moving. It is also helpful to keep similar items together. This works especially well for socks. For example, when I have an abundance of socks to keep together, we have a sock bucket. We go through the bucket once a month, and if we can't find a match, we get rid of them or find a reuse for them."
>
> —Diana Naramore, CEO of Sip & Ship, Seattle, Washington

What do you do if your child is emotionally attached to their items?

It all starts with a conversation at their level. Understanding why they have certain emotions about the item and the story they have attached to it. That story may surprise you. It may have been a special memory they are not ready to let go of, or they could just be demonstrating a strong possessiveness with things.

I'm not a psychologist *or a parent*, so please use your best judgement during this process. In my experience, taking the time to understand why children like certain things over others can be eye-opening and in stark contrast to our own views. Organizing can be such a bonding experience if done correctly.

Teaching your children to detach from physical belongings is foundational to having a healthy relationship with the environment around them.

Things change.

Things break.

Things serve a specific purpose at one time that may not at another.

Teaching them not to hold such strong feelings toward belongings will help them understand the cycle of stuff.

Give them an understanding of what is purposeful now. What currently has the most value and meaning in their life? These questions allow them to get into the habit of understanding what no longer serves them and how to move an item along in its cycle. The idea of simply discarding items as trash sets off an alarm. Children crave to understand that items have a cycle and often resist it when they don't see the benefit. If it's no longer fun for them, painting a picture to them that those items can go to another child who by donating to a charity, friend, or family member will be so excited to receive them.

What motivates kids to stay on task?

Kids love music. Ask them what they want to listen to. Crank it up and have fun with them! I was recently working with a client who was having trouble connecting with her preteen daughter. Her mother desperately pleaded with her every day to clean her room, but after a few months, her mother called me for help.

"I've tried everything to get her to clean her room," she said. "Any advice?"

I suggested that before we did anything, her daughter should pick her favorite music on my phone using Spotify. The look on her daughter's face went from extreme torture to game on!

I can listen to anything I want?
With the volume up?!

After just three hours, I had her room looking like something out of a PB2 magazine all while rocking out to Jojo Siwa. We found everything from lost money to birthday gifts and lost jewelry. She was so excited to take back her space. It was a fun bonding experience, too. She shared with me that it started to get hard for her to manage when her dresser broke and never was repaired. She stopped trying to keep it all together because when she would put it away, it all fell apart. All she needed was to be in her space and be reminded how cool organizing can be with a method, a positive attitude, and good music.

Classroom Structure

The difference between a tantrum and frustration is facts.
Do your kids *have* an organized system to put their items away?
Are receptacles labeled and easy for them to understand?

The key to keeping your child organized is to structure those spaces and systems like a classroom. You want to create specific zones for reading, sleeping, playing, and homework. If everything is everywhere, how can you expect your child to follow through?
The bedroom is a place to structure downtime and rest. Limit the number of toys and distractions. Use this space to organize books and start a routine of bedtime reading. Create an environment that settles the mind.

When a child walks into an organized classroom, there's routine and structure. Borrow that structure and implement the same system at home. Since these systems are repeated to children all day at school, it's best to not reinvent the wheel. Have things clearly labeled, at their height, and accessible.

When thinking about children's spaces you want to ask yourself the following questions.

- Can they reach it?
- Can they hook it?
- Can they bin it?
- Do they understand the labeling on the organized bin?

Masterpiece or Rough Sketch?

The thought of tossing a single item created by your little one can be too much. I assure you that your little Picasso will go on to make more beautiful masterpieces. Elementary school is a great time to teach balance with creative expressions. What's worth keeping are the masterpieces, everything leading up to that is practiced art. Nothing can compare to your most loved artwork, so why keep all that clutter?
Give your masterpiece the attention it deserves!

Technology can be your friend when it comes to storing artwork. Kids bring home projects by the truckload, and let's face it, some of it's awesome, but not every sketch is masterpiece. Over the last few years, I've taken the steps below and created cute little booklets, year by year, of every finger-painting, papier-mâché, and glitter-encrusted creation.

- For each year your child is in school making projects, keep one large bin of art.
- About once a month go through this bin alone, then with your little one.
- Make sure you are asking them to identify the pieces they truly love.

- Ask them what their favorite pieces are, then write their story on the back of the artwork.
- Thank your little one for their help and send them away.
- You're the editor and the publisher, so make any final cuts before you take the next step.
- Snap a photo of each art project from the bin and create a memory book to be digitally printed and enjoyed.

I've used a company called Chatbooks that imports all your Instagram photos into one cute little book for a great price with little to no effort. I love it! Artkive is also a great app where you can create a small book for each year of your child's art. Instead of hoarding all this stuff, you make a memory to leave out on the table for guests and family to enjoy.

Kids want to eat, learn, and play where you are.

I've had many clients try to get their kids to play in the basement and make that area seem really cool so that they won't be disruptive. The idea is that they can contain their children and their toys where no one will see them. Sometimes, it works. Most of the time, not so much.

Kids crave attention from their parents. They want to be where you are. Creating a space for them in your living areas makes them feel incorporated rather than isolated. I understand the need to keep your spaces aesthetically pleasing, but you can do so in a way that your kids can also be a part of.

In the living spaces, invest in storage ottomans that complement the décor. This way, kids can play with their toys, and it's a quick dump back into the ottoman for cleanup. Hall trees are wonderful for containing shoes, backpacks, and jackets. They look beautiful in the entryway and provide easy, organized storage. Large canvas bins with a windowed label can also be used to contain paperwork and art projects.

10 Questions to Help You Declutter Every Room in Your Home

When deciding what items to keep and what items to part with, having some careful self-talk is important. I've prepared a list of ten questions to ask yourself as you begin to declutter every room in your house.

1. Do I need this?
2. Does this make me feel happy?
3. Have I used this within the past year?
4. If I were out shopping, would I buy this?
5. Am I holding onto this for sentimental value?
6. Is this something I use regularly?
7. Do I feel obligated to keep this item?
8. Am I saving this item "just in case" I need it in the future?
9. Is this item worth the time and effort to keep, store, and maintain this item?
10. Could I use this space for something else by letting this go?

LESS IS MORE

PART TWO

6 | Clutter Isn't Cheap

"The price of anything is the amount of life you exchange for it."
-Henry David Thoreau

If the first chapters left you feeling overwhelmed at the thought of getting your life organized, that is completely normal. I first wanted to provide you with my secret sauce for getting the job done quickly using the Impact Organizing Method. Now, I want to ignite a serious fire under you to get motivated!

In this chapter, we're going to examine the high price of clutter. Can you afford to live the lifestyle of continual accumulation?

According to NAPO the National Association of Professional Organizers, the average person spends one year of their lifetime looking for lost items. Yikes!

Lateness

Although lateness is not a hereditary disorder, it can be a learned trait and I'm quite sure that my ability to be "tardy to the party" was passed down by my mother.

One of my favorite memories of my mother is of me sitting on the toilet, watching her get ready in the mornings for work. It took her a minimum of an hour to two hours if she was getting really done-up. Her routine always fascinated me. My mother is a beautiful woman who could always turn any head in the room, but it was always after she was fashionably late. She didn't realize that her power was in her confidence, not her makeup. Her personality fills any room regardless of her beauty routine.

It has taken me a long time to improve my lateness. I got so comfortable being late that my friends automatically started lying to me about what time to meet them so that I would be on time. What I know to be true for myself is that I had higher priorities than being on time. I had to start asking myself, "If I do this right now, will it cause me to be late for someone else?"

Once I actually looked at it, I felt guilty that I was placing other tasks in front of being committed to honoring others' time.

Was curling my hair crucial to today's event?
That took an extra fifteen minutes this morning.

Did that perfectly winged eyeliner really enhance my meeting today?

That took an extra fifteen minutes, too. You can see where these little pesky ideas take priority and our precious time.

What are you making a higher priority than being on time?
More sleep?
Your beauty routine?
Once you identify where your priorities lie, ask yourself why you value those things.

What kind of ripple effect does your being late have on the people around you?

How will showing up on-time or even early improve your day-to-day life?

Frustration

The Oxford dictionary defines frustration as the feeling of being upset or annoyed, especially because of the inability to change or achieve something. Your happiness is a high price to pay to be frustrated by clutter. How many times have you found yourself frustrated with not achieving an organized space? What if I told you that by cutting the clutter from your life, you'll instantly reduce stress and frustration? Seriously! We're always looking for the right product or the quick fix to making our lives easier and less frustrating.

Getting rid of the clutter in your life will eliminate that frustration—it's the magic pill you've been waiting for! If you're a self-aware individual who puts effort into starting your day with positivity as a priority, you have the knowledge to know that how you start your day predicates how the rest of your day flows.

Here are a few scenarios. In the first two, we see how clutter can lead to frustration. In the third, we see how you can conquer that frustration.

Scenario #1
Suzie's alarm goes off. She's annoyed by the sound and really tired, so she hits the snooze button five times. Now she only has a few minutes to wake up, so she scrambles to her

feet, only to feel the crushing sensation of stepping on her dog's chew toy.

The frustration hits two seconds into her morning.

Scenario #2
Suzie wakes up at the first sound of her alarm, puts her feet on the cozy clean floor, then walks to her bathroom and trips over her laundry basket. In the process, she stubs her toe so hard it takes her breath away. As she fights back tears of rage, she finally makes it to the bathroom.

The frustration hits two minutes into her morning.

Scenario #3
Suzie wakes up at the first sound of her alarm, puts her feet on the cozy clean floor, then effortlessly walks to her bathroom. She does her morning business and starts her morning coffee. She enjoys the smell of fresh brewed coffee as she completes her twenty-minute yoga session.

The difference?

The frustration and clutter have been eliminated.

Now, I'm not saying that things don't "pop up." If you can give yourself a beautiful start to your day, when little annoyances do hit, you'll be able to recognize that the frustration is not in line with your positive routine. Your approach will be one of clarity rather than frustration.

The "Closed-Door Room"

When I was growing up, we had a room just like this in our household. It is what I've named the "closed-door room." It was the room that no one was allowed to look at, speak of, or walk near. You'd be better off just not thinking about it at all. It was an unusable space that was so filled with miscellaneous clutter that you could barely find the light switch. This room caused continual emotional shame. Every time we needed something; it was in the closed-door room. Every time someone was coming over and there was anything laying out, it went into the closed-door room.

The Best Hidden Space In Your Home

Identify your "closed-door room." What area in your home is not usable? What could open up for you if this room were cleared of clutter? Take a few moments now and write down the area in your home that causes the most emotional shame. Once you have identified this space and how it currently makes you feel, I want you to dream. Dream of what you would want that space to look like, feel like, and smell like. Write what that room could be if you cut the clutter.

Thinking of Selling Your Home?

A cluttered home can be a devastating financial hit. I sat down with one of Seattle's top real estate agents, Erin Harold of Sotheby's Real Estate, to discuss the importance of a decluttered home and the impact it can have.

"When you're selling real estate for any reason, whether it's a $40,000 condo or if it's a $40 million property, it's all relatively the same thing that you're trying to do. And you're trying to make whatever it is you're selling look its very best. The most important thing you can do when preparing a property for sale is to depersonalize it. That means you have to take yourself out of the equation. You have to remove yourself emotionally from the property so that you can sell it. You have to remove all of your personal items from the home so that they don't interrupt someone else's vision of themselves coming into the space and living there."

Do you purchase duplicates because you lose things? When you can't find what you need, it often seems faster and easier to just buy a replacement. This is a financially dangerous habit that can really add up over time.

Do you lose a specific item often?
If so, how many conversations have your shared about losing that items?
Recognize the patterns and stop the cycle in its tracks. Think about how many things this week you've re-purchased.

Write that total down.
How many things this month have you re-purchased?
Write that total down.

After keeping these lists for a few months, you'll become aware of your clutter budget and how you can cut it from your life. If it helps, keep a log of anytime you re-purchase an item on your smartphone.

    You can also reverse the pattern by creating a consistent drop spot for quickly locating important items, such as your keys, phone, purse, and so forth. I typically like to keep them near the front of my home by the front door. That way, the first thing you do when you get home is drop your everyday items in the same consistent spot. The last action, of course, is to actually take consistent action. In order to start a productive pattern, you need to be consistent. Just like any healthy relationship, consistent, positive action is required for a successful partnership. If you're consistently putting your focus on your belongings and living with less, you're adding value to the items that you keep.

By valuing every item in your home for a specific function, you reduce your need to consume or repurchase items you already own.

Social Life

Are you embarrassed to have friends or family come to your home?
Roughly eighty percent of The Organizing Experts clientele initially call us for this reason. They're preparing for someone to come stay in their home, and their guest bedroom is a catchall for everything in the house. Oftentimes, you can't even *see* a bed.

Maybe you dream of entertaining a group or hosting a family dinner party. The social impact of clutter is far-reaching and often cuts deep into our self-esteem. For some of my clients, their home had become a point of contention within their family or social circle. Loved ones have become concerned for their well-being. Getting your home organized will not only make you feel more confident, it will also allow you to share your home and life with those you love.

Make Your Goals A Reality!

Grab a sheet of paper and write down the date you would like to have people over in large print at the top. Then, set a timer for five minutes. Under that date, describe what the event would look like.

Who will be there?
What are you serving?
In what room will this take place?
What does it feel like? What does it look like?

What Makes a House a Home?

If you're feeling like you would rather be anywhere than at your home, I'd like to help inspire you to think differently. For years, I've found myself going back home when the world seems too big for me to manage. My friends and I joke that Mema's house is like a vortex in time. It's a place where you will always feel at home, no matter what you do, who you become, or where you may go in the world. Mema's will be a constant source to replenish your soul and your calorie count.

Mema's house is so special to me. It's the one house without a single bare inch of free space—the one house I wouldn't change for all the money in the world. We often joke that when she passes, I'll board the doors so no one can take anything. That way, I can keep it as a museum forever!
It's completely rational, I know.
When talking to people who are stressed by their home, I love having the conversation of what they think makes a house a home?

Over the years, I've started to take little bits of what bring me joy in her home and implement them in my own. It's not a matter of decorating but creating little moments in your everyday life that calm you—moments that comfort you and make you feel at home. Sometimes, reflecting on your childhood helps you remember what lights you up from the inside. To my fortune, all I have to do is go to Mema's house for the reminder of what's really important. It' a place that's both ever-changing and never-changing.

At first glance, you wouldn't think anything of it. It's not a multi-million-dollar home adorned with the latest gadgets and upgrades. In fact, it's charmingly the opposite. It's a country chic pink and white home with a wooden swinging gate that links to my mother's house, where my best friend and I would run back and forth to catch the latest episode on Dawson's Creek and TRL back in 2001. It's where I spent most of my teens, twenties, and now my thirties. I always know a home-cooked meal and open arms will be waiting.

If you're trying to discover what home means to you, her, are some things that make Mema's house so charmingly special.

- At Mema's, the TV is always on. It's either Ghost Hunters, Golden Girls, or *Whose Line is It Anyway*
- Naps on her couches are not only okay but encouraged.
- If you want a frosty mug, there's always one waiting in the freezer.
- In the middle of conversation, you can expect Mema to sing a random song from any previous comment, followed by belly laughter so hard it hurts.
- A house full of girls from every generation running around and congregating in the shop, tweezing, applying makeup, painting nails, and back-combing their locks for the fun of it.
- Old photos (printed) and taped to every interior cupboard so that you can always stop to enjoy a

special moment from the past while you search for your favorite coffee mug.
- There will *always* be a fresh pot of strong coffee brewing in the morning.
- Everyone knows that we have a ghost in the house, and we all just go with it.
- Be it close to any holiday or not, Mema has décor up from every holiday at any point in time. Whether they light up, inflate, or flicker, her decorations fit perfectly.
- At Mema's, faith and family are built into the foundation of every conversation.

I share these memories with you because these are the details that make a house feel like home.

When you're stuck in the clutter, these special details can be hard to remember. I want you to take a moment and write out what feels like home to you.

What can you take from your childhood and bring into your home?

What makes a house a home is not about stuff. It's about the routines, smells, sounds, and the memories you make.

Downtime

Do you feel relaxed in your home at the end of a busy day? Or do you come home to a laundry list of things to accomplish when you walk through the door? When your home is in disarray, clutter is stealing your downtime. Instead of coming home to relax, you instead feel exhausted and frustrated trying to get your home in order. Home should be a place of healing, memories, and refuge. For so many of us, we get lost in the business of living that we forget to create a life. If you've forgotten what a relaxed breath feels like, maybe it's time for a change.

Having a home that supports your soul and comforts your mind is essential. If not in your home, where else are you going to seek comfort?

Something to examine is the energy you get from your home. Does the thought of going home depress you or excite you? The one thing that differentiates a house from a home is the love that's put into it. You shouldn't create an environment without love and intention. When you apply these two elements when deciding what to bring into your home and what needs to leave your home, you will find the decision-making process much easier. Love is what makes a house a home. If you don't love it, what is your intention behind purchasing an item or keeping an item?

Healing can begin at home.

Home is where the heart is. If you are looking around your current environment and feel that something is missing, have hope. One thing that is hardwired in every human is the ability to love. Start with any corner in your home and give it some love using the Impact Organizing Method.

Bills, Bills, Bills

According to Harris Interactive, twenty-three percent of adults pay their bills late because they lose them.[1] Autopay is a magical invention, but it takes some time to set up and some dedication to use. Many companies offer options for you to move your pay date and arrange for autopay.

---

[1] *Harris Interactive harris-interactive.com*

Begin by compiling a list of your bills by company and when the payment is due. Again, I would make a list that is quickly accessible via a note-taking app on your smart phone called "Master List for Bills." Next time you receive a statement, create your Master List.

Company	Amount	Due date

Now that you have your bills in a central list, you can arrange them by due date. Make a quick call to some of your debtors to see if you can align the "due date" so that most of your bills come out at the same time every month, possibly on autopay. This way you don't have to worry about losing a paper statement. If you are a bit savvier with using your phone for digital organization and reference, you may want to also list your account number and details. That way, if you have to call about one of your accounts, all the info is at your fingertips.

Time

"The hurrier I go, the more behinder I get."
—Lewis Carroll, Alice in Wonderland

Clutter has a deceptive way of stealing our time. Its objective is to distract you, frustrate you, and eat up your precious time. We all have the same twenty-four hours in our day as Beyoncé, yet we don't seem to be as "Sasha Fierce" as we'd like to be.

Time is our most precious asset. It's also the great gift that we can give. When we give someone or something our time, we're giving a portion of our lives we can never get back. You must make time for things that make your soul happy and be aware of what you're trading your life for. Taking the time to organize your home, room by room, and set a clear foundation of what works for you and your household will eliminate many stresses of day-to-day life. After your systems are in place, the only time you'll need to give to your system will be to maintain the order. Maintenance is far less time-consuming than constantly shuffling through the chaos.

7 | Tiny Home, Big Living

Think of your life with less. Less stress, less decisions, less stuff. Can you be happy in life with less? A few months before writing this book, I decided to Airbnb my home and really walk my talk to live with less. All my essentials had to fit into a large suitcase.

I challenged myself to live with less for a whole month, and it was quite an eye-opening experience. I noticed that I only wear about ten percent of my clothes, even if I have the choice of more options. Then, I reduced my personal and cosmetic products by eighty percent. I picked outfits that I knew would be comfortable and versatile given the occasion and weather conditions.

Instead of feeling like I had to be trendy, I stuck to the basics. I only fixed my hair in one of three ways and simplified my daily routine as much as possible. Even my makeup routine from 30 minutes down to the basics, just a bit of mascara and lip gloss.

I realized how much time I gained by having less distractions and options. In my mind, I was afraid what people would think of me living out of my suitcase. The truth is, no one noticed any difference.   They were shocked when I told them that I was living from a suitcase for a whole month. I received the same amount of outfit compliments as I did when I was frantically running around to keep up an image. My insecurities started to dwindle one-by-one. The people in my life who see me fully are not really looking at my outfit. A compliment is an offering and an invitation of kindness. A moment in time of offer to say, "I see you."

By simplifying my morning routines, limiting my options, and learning how to delay my gratification when I want something new, my world opened up to focus on the tasks and opportunities to connect with others that really mattered.

The Financial Impact of Clutter

Clutter is expensive. Whether it's taking up valuable space in your home or hitting you in your wallet when you make duplicate purchases or rent storage space, your extra stuff will run up your bills. The cost of clutter is very real and is one expense that can be cut altogether. To determine how much clutter is costing you, here's a quick little exercise to help put a price tag on it.

Calculate Your Clutter Cost

Take your home's value X, divided by the square footage Y. The product is the value of each square foot. Now you can determine how many square feet are unusable due to clutter and multiply by this number. This is what it costs to *store* your clutter.[2]

---

[2] *Lifehacker.com*

Example: A $300,000 home divided by 1,500 square feet = $200 per square foot. If your spare room is only storing clutter, the cost of your clutter could be as much as $40,000!

Do you use your garage to park your car or your clutter? Clutter is like an invasive weed. It starts out small and seemingly harmless, but it will take over your whole garden in the blink of an eye. In this case, clutter takes over our mental and physical space—space that we pay good money for. Sometimes our stuff takes up so much space in our home that we just move it to a new location. A storage unit. For many, clutter can seem debilitating. I've seen more "guest rooms" turned into "storage rooms" than I can count.

> "It's about making memories, because items can't go with you everywhere in a travel trailer. We live with only the essentials. It's been challenging but has taught me a lot. I've learned living with less is actually simple. My life is simple and I find so much comfort in that. I'm happy. I feel like I don't need things to make me happy. I've met so many people traveling. Instead of investing in decorating my walls, I've decorated my life with relationships and adventures."
>
> —Britnee Rogich

A Shift in Culture

Numerous facets of our culture have tainted our idea of modern living. I think a few things have ruined the idea of achievability in living like the Joneses. Reality TV and things that are made to look like reality have put "keeping up with the Joneses" so far out of reach that we go broke in the process.

Many people are adopting a new idea of living with less. They're finally beginning to ask themselves if bigger is really better.

Back in the early 2000s, MTV aired a show called MTV Cribs, a documentary type television program showcasing home tours of the rich and famous. In recent years, many reports have come to light that many of the celebrities featured didn't even own the cars or homes on the show.[3] It was completely fabricated to present an ideal to the viewer! You can't keep up with the Joneses and neither can the Joneses. (Or, apparently, Ja Rule.)

It's really thrilling to see recent American culture adopt a new idea in the opposite direction with minimalism and tiny homes. Going small is about sustainability and living large. I talked to Kurt Galley, owner of Carriage Houses NW, to discuss this movement toward minimalism and the desire to live "tiny."

Interview with Kurt Galley

I think there are two basic reasons why there is such a movement in minimalism. One is a very practical one. In our neck of the woods (Pacific Northwest), a massive percentage of the population is just priced out of the housing market. You have people who practically cannot buy a traditional home, and they don't just want to throw $2,000 a month at rent. So, looking at small and tiny options opens up the possibility of ownership. There are a lot of people in it.

There are people nearing retirement who don't have a big enough nest egg to have a home and be retired, so they are

---

[3] https://www.thethings.com/shady-facts-about-mtv-cribs-people-keep-ignoring/

selling, putting it into cash, and putting it into small or tiny. And you have young people who are looking at down payments and monthly payments that they can't even fathom and are considering tiny. And then you have the others who are independent of all that so they're making the decision that they want to go tiny and be minimalist.

So, it may not be a practical, but a conscious choice to stay small, have a small carbon footprint, get rid of stuff, and commit to a very minimal lifestyle has great benefits. Those people have a certain demographic. They tend to be people who are active, outdoorsy, want to get out and have adventures, and don't want to be tied down to a mortgage, a house, or things they have to take care of that stack up their to-do list every week. They just want to be freed up to blow with the wind.

The bottom line?
People don't want to be owned by their stuff.

It's a response to an economic reality and to a growing consciousness that you are not measured by your 4,200-square-foot home. Ten years ago, someone who wanted to let you know that they were doing pretty well might throw the size of their house into the first few sentences of a conversation. But I don't think it's in vogue to lead with that now. It might be the opposite. People might brag that they live in 400 square feet.

A young woman came in had been journaling her path to tiny. She was a PhD student, and the shift was part of her dissertation. She started journaling her life experiences and focusing on her happiness level. When she first started it, she lived in a 2,800-square-foot house, and she downsized three times, cutting each new space down by nearly half its size. She went down to 1,200 square feet, then 800. 800 square feet led to 400, which eventually went down to a tiny house.

As she went back through her journals, she got happier every time she downsized. Every time she gets rid of stuff, she becomes happier in the process. For me, that was a real eye-opener. It's a real-world example of someone who committed to cleaning out her life.

The more I purge, the smaller my footprint. The smaller my footprint, the less space I consume. When my consumption of space lessens, my joy increases.

8 | Health Impacts of Clutter

The correlation between our health and clutter has been gaining a lot of attention. After a day of organizing, my clients tell me that a huge weight has been lifted off their shoulders. You may not realize the heavy weight of clutter you've been carrying—be it emotional or physical. I know for sure that any form of decluttering will lighten your load.

> "Nutrition has a lot of organization to it. I think from the science of how food works in our bodies that our body is naturally organized, to the meal planning and the prepping. It takes foresight of going to the store and what you're making and what you're getting and what you're skipping. So, organization is a huge part of it."
>
> —Cynamon Quinton Heide

My friend Peter Walsh says there's a link between the clutter in our homes, increased stress, and weight gain. He writes about it in his book, Lose the Clutter, Lose the Weight.[4]

---

[4] *Lose the Clutter, Lose the Weight: The Six-Week Total-Life Slim Down* by Peter Walsh

If your mind continues to force you to overeat, over-shop, and hang on to household items long after they've stopped being useful, your body won't be able to exercise and declutter fast enough to keep up. If your mind continues to be unhappy, overstressed, and unfocused, your drive to maintain your improvements will fade. To make deep, lasting changes to the appearance of your body and home, you're going to have to use your mind differently than before.

When it comes to groceries, we also have a habit of buying things we already have at home when we leave the house without a list. Madeline Eyer, raw food coach and owner of Consciously Raw, puts it this way.

Conscious living goes hand in hand with conscious eating. It is a way of being that permeates all aspects of life. Having an organized kitchen is essential. It prevents you from buying ingredients that you already have in the back of the cupboard and ensures that you have fresh ingredients on hand when you need them. Knowing what you have in stock or simply looking before you shop can prevent you from spending money you don't need to spend. Creating a list can also keep you from buying those unhealthy food choices. If you are eating consciously, then by extension you are going to live consciously and make choices that are conscious. It is a way of being that permeates you.[5]

Clutter and Stress

According to a study in the Personality and Social Psychology Bulletin, people with cluttered homes full of unfinished

---

[5] **https://www.consciouslyraw.com/**

projects were more depressed, fatigued, and had higher levels of the stress hormone cortisol than those who described their homes as "restful" and "restorative."[6]

Do you love window shopping?

Are you already dreaming of something newer or better than what you have right now?

The constant need for more things puts you in a place of never finding contentment with what you already have.

Do you really need more shoes, designer jeans, and a perfectly Pinterest home right now?

Challenge yourself to be in a state of gratitude and observe the stress of needing more fade to the background.

Simplify Your Diet Choices

I have to admit, I'm an emotional eater. Shopping for groceries or feeding myself has been a challenge.

In my interview with nutritionist Meagan Lindquist, she gave me some simple ideas for a healthy lifestyle on the go.

> My go-to that I would bring with me is veggies. Overdose on veggies! Carrots, snap peas, broccoli. You could also bring hard-boiled eggs, or you could do nuts. Nuts are great because they

---

[6] https://undecidedthebook.files.wordpress.com/2012/07/saxbe-repetti-pspb-2010.pdf

are really filling, and the healthy fats will hold you over for a while. The Instant Pot is great because it is super quick! There is a setting for one-minute quinoa. Usually it takes about thirty minutes on the stove. Another reason I like the Instant Pot is grains have certain proteins around them called lectins, which are really hard to digest, and over time that can build up and cause clutter in our bodies, but the Instant Pot uses such high heat and pressure, it breaks down the hard-to-digest proteins. Even with small changes like this, you are going to feel better, you are going to look better, and you are going to crave the things that make you thrive, not just survive.

Clutter Triggers Respiratory Issues

As more things pile up, more dust is generated, and this environment is an ideal place for dust mites to multiply. According to the Alliance for Healthy Homes, cluttered homes often contain more dust, which can cause or amplify breathing problems.[7] The accumulation of pet dander from dogs and cats also contributes to allergy symptoms and makes breathing more difficult.

When things are piled on the floor, it makes cleaning harder to achieve. Your cluttered environment can also be confusing to your pets, and they will be more prone to having accidents that can cause serious damage to your home and your health. Cat urine specifically contains a particularly high concentration of ammonia. In the same way pleasant scents improve our mood, bad smells can also make us unhappy and irritable. The harder it gets to access different

---

[7] Alliance for Healthy Homes
www.hometowndumpsterrental.com/blog/health-effects-of-a-cluttered-home

areas of the home to clean, the more serious these respiratory issues can become.

Hoarding and Your Health

> "Generally, from my aspect of others with a hoarding disorder, they can't use their kitchen to cook, their bathroom to go to the bathroom in, or a bed to sleep on. They're sleeping on their sofa on a pile clothes. When it starts taking over your life and you don't let people come to your house because you're embarrassed or it starts taking over your personal life, then that's hoarding."
>
> —Scott Barkley, Bio Decon Solutions

In 2009, my first and last hoarding client was referred to me by the local fire department. She had suffered a heart attack the week prior, and the first responders were unable to enter through the front door. When they abandoned attempting entry though the front door, they found a side door and had to clear a path to find her and get her on a gurney and out of the house. They told her if she didn't seek help, there wouldn't be a next time. She would more than likely die trapped in her home surrounded by clutter.

The Mental Health Association of San Francisco warns that excessive amounts of clutter—especially cardboard boxes, paper, and clothing—can block doorways and windows, creating a serious fire hazard.[8]

I have an elastic heart, so when I heard this story, I immediately felt I had to help.

---

[8] Mental Health Association of San Francisco www.mentalhealthsf.org/what-are-some-consequences-of-having-too-much-clutter

That was a learning lesson for everyone.

Many objects were thrown at me and I was cursed out more times than I can remember. I was intuitive enough to duck and cover as an empty pill bottle whizzed by my head. She called me at 2 a.m. because she couldn't find her TV guide and accused me of hiding it from her. As I'm trying to rationalize the situation and calm her nerves, she rolled over to the other side of her bed and found her TV guide, on her nightstand.

She was so distraught with the openness of her new clean surroundings she didn't know how to function. She had never been able to see the other side of her bed before, let alone the entirety of her room for *years*. It was a shock to her system and daily routines.

That may be a "TV-worthy" moment, but the reality is, you can only help someone who is mentally not ready for change and they must make the decision to get help *themselves*.

"When you get organized, your whole life avails itself to you in a new way, because it doesn't seem so bleak. Clutter makes your life seem bleak and unattainable, resulting in hopelessness and despondency. When you declutter and get organized, you see your life in a new light. That light is hope. For a person who hoards, whatever compulsion that they are giving into, or whatever ritual they are exercising each day, that is them trying not to suffer. As humans, we are just trying not to suffer. Period."

—Erica DiMiele, Expert on A&E's hit show, Hoarders

*If you or someone you know is in need of hoarding help, we have a great local reference for you in the back of this book.

The Bitter Roots of Hoarding

What void are you trying to fill with stuff?

Does having stuff make you feel comforted?

I've met people who felt less lonely because the stuff piling around them was a sense of comfort, much like a security blanket. I, too, have succumbed to retail therapy.

I was going through a really hard breakup and I wanted to be anywhere but home. This relationship was showing signs of trouble I didn't want to acknowledge, and I found refuge at HomeGoods. It was my new love. I soon began an unhealthy habit with Pinterest and soothed myself with a shopping trip.

I don't know what it is about Target and HomeGoods that is so magical, but just being in the store and imagining all the possibilities, even if only for an hour, allowed me to escape the reality waiting for me at home. A chapter of my life that I didn't ever want to end was ending. We all have something that we need to escape from at times in our life. They call it retail therapy for a reason.

How does it feel?

A shopping addiction typically starts with a feeling of tension or arousal when thinking about going shopping. Next comes a strong urge to shop and buy for the temporary feelings of relief during the act of buying. According to the Verywell psychology website, once a purchase is made, feelings of guilt soon follow.[9]

As with other types of addictions, there are cravings—feelings so strong and exciting that they're frequently uncontrollable—and the shopping addict will ignore the negative consequences that might come from buying, such

---

[9] **www.verywellmind.com**

as angering a spouse, bouncing a check, having a credit card declined, or not having money for necessities. As with any repetitive behavior or signs of addiction, the first step to overcoming these issues is giving them respect and recognizing their existence in your life. The next best step is to ask yourself how the addiction makes you feel in the long term.

When we acquire things to fill a void, the feelings of happiness are temporary. You can't solve a long-term issue with impulsiveness. Delaying gratification is a practice that will open so much space in your life and your bank account.

Is this just clutter, or am I hoarding?

There's a very real difference between someone who has clutter and someone who is struggling with hoarding habits. For the individual whose clutter constricts their daily activities such as bathing, cooking, or sleeping fall into a category of hoarding. I sat down with hoarding expert Erica DiMiele to examine the complexity of hoarding and understand why people hoard items.

> It comes down to security and insecurity. Consumers in our society adopt this scarcity mindset, that there is not enough to go around for everybody—work, business, clients, whatever—so we hoard them. We hold on because they're ours. We're just humans trying not to suffer. Period. For a person who hoards, whatever compulsion that they are giving into, or whatever ritual they are doing every day, is just them trying not to suffer. The willingness, a willing heart, and a humble heart to admit where you're at, and that you do need some assistance, as we all do in different ways, I feel is the number one piece of advice. Public

shaming others who struggle with clutter has become popular in our recent culture. Individuals who are considered a 'hoarder' have also been labeled as less than or viewed as incompetent. Please understand that at the heart of the issue is a human who is hurting.

The level of hoarding is typically an outward display of an internal struggle. People say, 'I need help with my hoarding.' No, you need help with why you are hoarding things. What we find is that when we give things away, really let go, and cut the clutter, our world opens up a little bit, our home unveils itself, and our human relationships become better, deeper, and fuller because we are not saturated in our crap all the time.

What should we take away from this?

- Understand what you're filling your life with and *why*?
- How does clutter make you feel?
- Looking at the cause of the clutter in your life.
- Examine the behavior and intention of acquiring items.
- Why we should collect moments and not things.
- How the acquiring possessions makes you feel.
- Understand what hoarding is and why it's a growing epidemic in American culture.
- Think about why living with less leads to so much more.

9 | Clutter at Work

For most of us, our waking hours are spent working. Imagine if your workplace was filled with inspiration and served as an incubator for taking your work to the next level. It may seem like a far-fetched idea that our workspace can cultivate anything but a never-ending flow of paperwork, but I believe that an organized work environment can shift an entire company. Think about it. When a fish gets sick, you don't treat the fish. You treat the water. Our environment shapes our day-to-day experience and sets the stage for growth. It can also hold you back if it's full of clutter.

> "I try my best every day—but I'm just a one-woman show over here! The biggest thing for me is staying on top of emails and having systems in place to organize all my to-dos. I think the best practice for staying organized is having everything in one place that you can come back to and finding the best systems that work for you. I take really great pride in being a great communicator, under promising/overdelivering, and staying on top of it all. I find that I'm able to stay organized because I choose to make it a priority in how I run my business."
>
> —Michelle Moore, Portrait & Lifestyle Photographer

The workplace is my favorite place to organize. Even as a child, I would get so excited to go to work with my mom. I felt like the most privileged kid on the planet when my mom could take me to her office. At the time, she was in the National Guard and being allowed to go on base with her always felt like a big deal. Her office was always tidy and organized and had a large organized shrine of me tacked to her cubical wall. On special occasions, I got to help her with her administrative tasks of alphabetizing paperwork or tearing the perforated edges off the printer paper. (*If you don't know perforated printed edges are, I feel old.*)

> "PPP: prior planning prevents piss poor performance."
> —Kelly

Getting Organized at Work

A CareerBuilder study found that twenty-eight percent of employers are less likely to promote someone with a messy workspace.[10] Whether you work at a corporation or run your own operation, having an organized space allows you to focus on the task at hand. You don't want to miss out on opportunities and stress about the clutter that surrounds your office space. Researchers from the National Institute of Mental Health discovered compulsive hoarding was associated with an average of seven work impairment days per month—more than those reported by participants with other anxiety, mood, and substance use disorders.[11]

Having designated systems and spaces for mail, filing, projects, and goals sets the stage for success. Being organized

---

[10] Careerbuilder.com
[11] Researchers from the National Institute of Mental Health www.ncbi.nlm.nih.gov/pmc/articles/PMC3018686

not only builds your own confidence—it shares that confidence with those around you.

In this chapter, we will discuss the Impact Organizing Method and look at the top five areas to organize your work environment to boost your mood and productivity in the workplace.

1. Desk Space

Your work environment should be set up in three zones. You should have a place for projects, a place for you archives, and a place for your references. Start by clearing the floor space and any cords or debris that could interfere with your electronics or outlets. Examine your desktop and its function. Too often, our desktop serves the function of all three zones. Starting from the left side of your desk and moving to the right, categorize and group like items together, keeping paperwork together in one large pile. Then, establish where items need to live.

Do you have a working foundation to store your items?

Your desk space should be clear of clutter and only contain your essentials for working on tasks. This makes it easy for you to tidy up at the end of your workday and ensures you have a clear workspace for the next day. Items such as books, binders, and manuals need to be in a reference zone so you can access them when needed. Again, you are keeping only the essentials you need at your fingertips on your desk.

2. Paperwork

Sticky notes are wonderful, but they are only to be used as temporary markers. Start centralizing your thoughts in one specific notebook. When it comes to making an impact by getting a handle on paperwork, start with the entire surface space (left to right) and gather all paperwork into one pile. Once you have your pile, delegate each piece to your system.

3. File Systems
Don't have a file system or know where to start? Create a basic filing system for your desktop and one for archival paperwork. Archive paperwork is not in your prime real estate spots. Typically, this is where paperwork goes to die, only to be referenced periodically—if ever. Things like taxes go into the archival system.

Your basic desktop system should be three files:
Projects > 5-min items > 30-min items > 1-hr items.
People often make the mistake of making a "to-do" category. The problem with this type of organization is that nearly everything is a "to-do."
By breaking tasks up into things that:
Take 5 minutes > 3 minutes > 1 hr.

This will help you quickly act on the less time-consuming projects first.

Having an IN/OUT box is also essential when it comes to organizing papers. You can use hanging file folder tabs for large categories and manila folders for subcategory items.

4. Digital Clutter
Digital clutter is the same, if not worse, than physical clutter! Just because it's digital, it often gets more cluttered than our physical space. Digital organization needs the same time and attention as physical clutter. I recommend using an online platform such as Evernote to keep everything organized and accessible. The concept is the same as organizing physical paperwork, but everything happens online. You can create notebooks (large category), items, and notes within each notebook. Google also has a ton of online digital platforms for organizing your online needs.

5. Email

Just because it doesn't take up physical space doesn't mean it isn't clutter. Your inbox clutter can be just as bad, if not worse, than physical mail. Get less email by taking ten minutes at a time to unsubscribe to those junk mailing lists. Flag the emails that are most important and delete the rest. Just red flag it or trash it. Each day, work on getting your red-flagged emails down to zero.

Less is More

When it comes to your office space, keep it minimal. You are there to perform a task. I know many people go all out and decorate their cubicle, and I've gotten lots of pushback from some employees. Decorating your cubicle is like building a museum of all the things that you'd rather be doing than being where you are right in your cubicle life.

Why not rock your cubicle with clear confidence?

"Back when the recession hit in 2008, a friend of mine launched a challenge. It was called 'the great American apparel' diet. We were on a walk, and we made a pact. We would not buy any new clothes for a year. The exception was undergarments and accessories. It was an opportunity to save money, time, and be creative with how you use what you already own. Many people said, 'How can you do that? You are a retailer and going against the grain.' That was a really good way to actively reduce my consumption and help the bottom line. I still do that today. Before I put something in my cart, I remember the experience and how valuable it was for me."

—Diana Naramore, CEO of Sip & Ship, Seattle, Washington.

The Organized Entrepreneur

As a teenager merging into the workplace, I remember the first time I was inspired by an office space. It was 2006, and I was in transition from my job as a telephone operator for NC Machinery. Back in the day, Craigslist hadn't really taken off and social media wasn't consuming our lives. Looking for work began with a polished resume, networking the old-fashioned way and knocking on doors of actual buildings.

Since I was only nineteen at the time, I didn't have much experience to glean from, but I knew that I wanted to be of service to others. I printed my MapQuest directions, and they led me to a specialist who could help me craft my resume and prepare for an interview. It was a little building with a small waiting room and small offices located inside. Nothing remarkable to speak of.

It wasn't until a young girl in her twenties led me from the waiting room back into her office space. All I could comprehend from that meeting was that she had a furry, zebra print office chair, and I couldn't understand how her boss allowed her to have that!

For starters, I learned she was already her own boss. Her walls were painted a soft pastel purple, and it was by far the trendiest thing I'd ever seen. I was forever changed. This was before Pinterest was born, and for years, I craved a personalized office space to look forward to visiting every day.

Fast forward a decade. Now I spend a good portion of my work talking to large companies and college universities about maximizing their potential in the workplace. In 2010, there was a big shift in companies like Google and Microsoft. They began embracing flexible and fun lifestyles centered around innovation and motivation. Whether you spend your working hours in a cubical or in a windowless closet with a custom-made tiny desk (actually happened to me), you can make an impact and be inspired by your workspace.

Operations

If you're self-employed, being organized on the go seems to require a whole lot more intention. No one is there to hold you accountable or create a system for you. The freedom to create whatever we want with our time and space is the big perk of the gig and can also be the most daunting. Some days, from the moment I wake up, my heart races just thinking of all the balls I need to juggle to keep the lights on.

Spending the time and budget to start off with a great foundation of creating and documenting your systems is the key to longevity in your career as an entrepreneur.

Besides using the Impact Organizing Method to organize the top five physical areas of your work environment, it's essential to create an operations binder for your company. This makes training your new hires much more effective, and everyone in your company will benefit from the clarity of codified expectations. Make sure to create space for phone calls, deskwork, paperwork, creativity, and planning. You want everyone working in your space to have structure and expectations. When you have clutter in your workspace and your lines of communication, it leads to unmet expectations and frustration within your team.

Task Management

Procrastination is real! If you feel like the hardest part of a project is simply getting started, try using the Five-Minute Rule. While it's true that our attention spans are steadily shrinking, concentrating on something for only five minutes is a cinch.
Take the approach Dr. Andrea Bonior describes in The Huffington Post.

We're scared of the big, amorphous blob of a task precisely because it IS so big and ill-defined, and because we worry that it will take two hours or two days to get to the bottom of it. And so we wallow.
We don't even open the envelope to that bill we have to negotiate, or we don't even unzip that suitcase we have to unpack, or we don't even take two minutes to assess the piles we have to organize and figure out how many categories to sort them into. But it's those small openings and un-zipping that in many ways are the biggest psychological barriers of all.

If you conquer them—doable in just a couple of minutes—and then you force yourself to stop after just that incremental progress, your energy and momentum will have started to flow. You might not even want to stop. And—here is another reason why the rule is so great—it will make you much more likely to come back to that task when you try for another five minutes (or perhaps you allow yourself ten or twenty) in the next day or so.
So, just tell yourself you can do five minutes. You absolutely can. It's not nearly as scary as an hour or an all-nighter. Whether it's writing that first paragraph or just ordering the book that you're supposed to be reading, that first step truly begins the bulk of the progress in getting there.

Impactful Tips for an Organized Workspace

- Have a personal goal to always end the day with a clear desk.
- Keep your workspace professional and personal items to a minimum.
- Have a basic filing system that sits on your desk for everyday projects and file away papers for archival storage.
- Understand what documents to keep and for how long while also knowing when to toss.
- Have your goals front and center so that you can look at them every day.
- Make sure everything you own has a home.

10 | Creating a Partnership Without Clutter

We all hold different emotional attachments to items and reading through this book will lend advice on how you can cut the clutter from your life. However, if you're living with a partner, friend, or family member, their attachment to items may be very different from yours. Are you and your partner on the same page when it comes to getting organized?

The biggest mistake that I see couples make is assuming how the other person feels about something. They then go about making decisions for the other person. This always leads to a resentful state. It's always best to never assume anything. Make sure you have clear communication with anyone you're living with about your expectations and why you feel strongly about having an organized home. If your home is going to stay organized, everyone involved needs to be on the same page.

When clients ask us to organize for someone else, we always ask the following questions.

- Will they be present for making decisions?
- Who is the chief decision-maker in the household?
- How do they feel about getting organized/downsizing?

You can only help someone get organized when they are ready. Going into a shared space and decluttering items that are not yours without permission is extremely violating. Our home and the contents within it are personal. This process demands care and respect. Having a conversation around the common goal of living with less is the first step. Have an open heart and an open mind. You may learn something new about your partner simply by having a meaningful conversation about the concept of living life with less, together.

What Happens When My Space Becomes *Our* Space?

It's common for partners to have different organizing styles. The important thing is finding common ground and coexisting in your space. It's an exciting time when you move in with someone new. Well, it should be.

If you're in the beginning of merging households, you may want to consider decluttering each household separately before the merge. Spend time itemizing your belongings room by room. Together, go through the list and evaluate duplicates so you can discuss who will take what. Make a list of items you want to keep and a list of the items you want to give away, donate, or sell. The goal is to have a manageable amount of stuff you want to keep that will fit the new shared space.

It's also helpful to know who will be responsible for certain revolving household tasks like getting the mail, doing laundry, and other mundane chores. Divide the household tasks according to what each person finds more favorable. If you do most of the grocery shopping and cooking, then it may be a good opportunity for your partner to help with putting away and cleaning up after meals. For other household chores, you can share the responsibilities, like cleaning the bathrooms or vacuuming the floors.

> "Consistency is the most important factor. We eliminate arguments by having less distraction or conversations around the how-to of what needs to be done. I have our refrigerator labeled, for example, to keep consistency. It's an area that is frequently used, and it's important to keep it organized in a way that works for both of our personalities. That way, whoever is putting items away, it's less about the how-to and more about the consistency of where they routinely go. We understand each other's needs, and so it opens the door to more quality communication about living organized. We can both walk into a room and decide what works as a team. It's never just a 'my way or the highway' mentality. We always come up with a plan together on what works for our home."
>
> —Jessica Clark, Organizing Expert

What's Your Organizing Style?

Not all organizing solutions work for all people! Discover your individual organizing personality. When merging households, I advise getting to know your partner's organizing style. Everyone's personal version of what is clean or organized is very different. What may seem tidy to you may throw your partner into a state of instant panic. It's important to understand what your organizing style is.

Important Factors of an "Open Style"

This organization style is typically that of a highly creative person who prefers to have easy and basic containment. Out of sight is out of mind for this personality. They often feel overwhelmed when they can't visually see their items. These individuals gravitate to clear containers with large category labels and are more concerned with functionality than uniformity.

- Clear Containment

Keeping items contained so they can still see the contents within is important for this organizational style.

- Items within reach

When items such as pills and vitamins are in a bin in the cupboard, they become forgotten about and will be less likely to be utilized. Having these items contained on a counter visually is important.

- Simple Systems

Having large categories is enough for this personality. Having subcategories and complex systems is just too overwhelming to maintain. For example, having home paperwork organized into just three to five categories would be sufficient.

- Bins

Bins are favored by this organizational style. You don't have to worry about the contents within them as long as they find their way to the appropriate bin.

Things That Are Important for a "Systematic Style"

Individuals who fall under the systematic organization style crave a high level of efficiency. They tend to gravitate to a more minimal lifestyle yet aspire to have every item contained and labeled in detail. These individuals gravitate to color-coded systems, subcategories, and attractive aesthetics. They get overwhelmed by the sight of clutter.

- Clear surface spaces

Keep surface spaces like the kitchen counter, nightstands, and bathroom sinks free of clutter.

- Permanent label systems

Create a permanent label system. The systematic stylist is the kind of person who would be on Etsy looking for the trendiest labeling system to organize her toddler's closet. Once a system is established, it needs to stay consistent.

- Uniformity in color and products

When looking for containment products, this organizing style wants uniformity and organizational products that are aesthetically pleasing. Having matching hangers that are all the same style and color in their closet would be important to this individual. Also, finding baskets or bins that complement their environment (such as an ottoman that doubles as storage) provides containment that fits the home aesthetically. Having plastic bins or clear storage is not favored by this personality type.

- Deeper separation of items

I often refer to this as the next level of organizing. Like an onion, you have to peel off the outer layer and work your way into the good part. The same is true for getting organized, starting with your first layer and then applying further organizational systems. Deep separation is important. A "junk drawer," for example, will drive this personality nuts. They would much prefer to have every space subcategorized.

Partner Prime Time

The most important thing to discuss is how you are priming each day for yourself and your partner. Taking time in the morning and evening is essential so that physical, mental, and emotional clutter doesn't become between you and your partner.

> "This is actually my husband's (Dr. Alan Christianson) technique. Oftentimes, we women have a hard time going to sleep and getting good quality sleep because we wake up in the middle of the night. And it's usually because we have brilliant ideas, or we remember things we have to do. He suggests doing a 'brain dump' before you go to sleep. Turn off all your electronics an hour before bedtime. Write down your entire to-do list then. When you turn off electronics, your mind is in creative mode because there aren't any distractions. This is the best time to 'dump' everything on paper so you can wake up refreshed because you know you haven't forgotten anything."
>
> —Kirin Christianson, Co-Founder, Integrative Health

11 | The Closet Audit

I have spent a lot of time in the closet. Hours of my life have gone to swapping out ugly wire hangers, folding mounds of clothing, and helping my clients decide which black shirt out of thirty they like best.

The closet is by far my favorite place to organize. Having a perfectly curated closet with clothes that make you feel your best, having organized labeled bins, and aligning shoes by style puts a warm feeling in my soul. I believe any closet space has the potential to be great given a few basic rules.

In this chapter, I've packed in all the good stuff. I'm going to give you five things you can get rid of right now that will make a huge positive impact on your life.

> "There are so few things in life you can control. Most things in life we cannot control. One small thing that you can control for yourself is what you buy and what you wear. You can control that. What you spend your money on, what you own, what you choose to wear... You have a lot of control there. I think when people's closets are out of control, it is a genuine pain point for them."
>
> —Darcy Camden, Styled Seattle Personal Shopping & Wardrobe Styling

Getting dressed should complement your body and how you feel. If something you put on makes you, for one second, feel uncomfortable or less than, take it off. We only have precious moments in our day, and we can't afford to waste any of them first thing in the morning worrying about what to wear.

What Holds Most People Back

You may fear that if you clean out your closet, you'll have no clothes left to wear. Personally, I would rather have one trusted pair of great fitting jeans than a stack reminding me of how skinny I used to be or need repair. Women in particular have a hard time of letting go of clothing.

While I get that this is just clothes and that there's more to life than clothes, I do think there's significance in how you start the day. How you enter the world and how you feel when you're moving through your day is important to your wellbeing.

Here are some common pushbacks.

Client: That was really expensive!
Kammie: The only real value of something is how much someone else is willing to pay for it. Right now, it's just hanging in your closet collecting dust. If you're finding it hard to get rid of clothes because of the price tag, you have a couple options.

- Stop buying expensive clothes that aren't staple, classic items.
- Expensive clothes just mean you don't like cheap clothes.

Client: I'm not at my ideal weight...

Kammie: As a woman, I can relate to bodies that are ever changing. We can only embrace our curves—not fight them. While it may be appropriate to keep a few clothes while you're in-between sizes, keep it realistic and organized. Keep and begin to curate clothing that makes you *feel* your best.

I want you to feel your best in the body you're in right now. You deserve to feel amazing today. Organize your clothes so that what fits now is easily accessible and those that are a size off are stored away. If those items have not been used within the next year, have another audit.

Client: That is my wedding dress from my previous marriage.

Kammie: What the what? That tells me you're looking at a garment of the past rather than the present. If you can't imagine the thought of parting with such a treasured article of clothing, determine if you can incorporate, pass it along or store it in such a way that gives it the respect and leaves the guilt behind.

For you, it might not be a wedding dress, but we've all got the skeletons of the past hanging in our closets.

- My friend/sister gave me that.
- I can't get rid of it!
- My mother-in-law will haunt me if I throw that out!

I still keep my grandfather's old ratted jacket that still smells like Benson & Hedges 100's. If it's a fond memory you want to honor, place it in a spot that's more accessible so you can see it every day. Moments are worth collecting and honoring, not hoarding for the sake of having. Try moving special pieces like this to the front of your coat closet rather than the back. Honoring special pieces in cases or frames is also a fun way to decorate your closet space. Look for little moments that can make a significant impact in your morning routine.

Seasonal Audit

I recommend doing a seasonal audit on your wardrobe. Assess what clothes you wore during that given season and audit them. Eliminate everything you didn't wear.

Closet Audit Essentials

Boost your confidence with these quick essentials to make an impact in your closet space. I've dedicated an entire chapter to organizing your closet because I believe that it's one of the most important spaces in your home to focus on. It sets the tone for the whole day. This is also the area that prepares you or depletes you first thing in the morning.

Here's how to make sure your closet is working for you.

- Streamline your hangers.
- If you have a lot of shelving space, adding canvas labeled bins to   keep them tidy.
- Give yourself a wardrobe hook for curating your outfits.
- Organize your shoes by style/color at eye level.
- Face all your clothing the same way.
- Organize clothing either by color blocking or length, then by color.
- Keep clothing fresh by using dryer sheets in drawers or bins.
- Invest in a full-length mirror.
- Good lighting doesn't have to be expensive. A battery-operated   motion light works miracles in dark spaces.
- Store shoes, accessories, and handbags in the same space.

- Add a belt loop to organize belts and keep a spare lint roller on hand.
- Foam noodles can keep your boots standing at attention.
- Have a handheld steamer ready for wrinkle care.

One of my favorite movies growing up was Clueless. The fashion, catch phrases, and Cher's closet were iconic in their own right. In the movie, she had a computer system for picking out her outfits. I mean, who wants to dig through a bunch of clothes? As if! Channel your inner Cher by mounting an old iPad to your closet. Download Pinterest for everyday style inspiration and effortlessly take notes on essential items you may need to replace or add to your wardrobe.

A Styled Closet Sets the Tone for Success

Now that we've decluttered some essentials, I want to give you my expert tips to styling your closet. From rock stars to desperate housewives. Believe me when I say that styling your closet is a MUST!

Once all your hanging clothes are on uniformed hangers, move to *styling* your closet. In other words, you want your closet to shop like a boutique. Each morning you arrive at your closet, your system should greet you with a "Hello, gorgeous!" Let's get dressed vibe.

You also want all your clothes to face you. When you walk to your closet, you should see the front of your clothes. Not all catawampus. All garments should face the same direction.

I love to use a color blocking technique when organizing closets. From tank tops to dresses, I organize by color, shortest to longest. This gives your closet a fresh boutique feel.

I also like to include my accessories in this space. I prefer to use a travel hanging jewelry organizer in my closet. That way, I can piece together my entire outfit from head to toe.

Finally, I always have a wardrobe hook nearby. This allows me to organize my outfits for the week. It's also a great dedicated spot for steaming garments. Outfit prep will save you so much time. After your closet audit and styling, getting ready in the morning will be something you'll look forward to.

There are five things in your closet you can discard to make a dramatic impact.

1. Funky Old Hangers

The key to an organized closet is uniformity. Matching hangers are the basic essential in keeping the flow of the closet. If you are looking at your closet and the hangers are all different sizes, materials, or colors, it just adds to the chaos. If you have clear, plastic department store hangers matched with dry-cleaning hangers and everything in between, nothing flows right.

If you take the time to swap out all your hangers for one specific type and color, facing the same way, you'll find that shuffling through them becomes much easier. Having the right type of hanger is important. Not everyone is a good match for those lovely velvet hangers. In my experience, men prefer either wooden or plastic slim hangers. Women, in my experience, tend to pick a slimmer hanger to maximize space in their closet and to properly hang more delicate tops that will slip off traditional hangers. Dry-cleaning should be taken off the temporary wire hanger once you bring it back to the closet. When you don't take off your dry-cleaning wrapping, it can also make it difficult to remember what exactly is in there.

Did you know that if you take in your dry-cleaning already on your preferred hanger, most dry-cleaning companies will return it the same way? No more wire hangers!

2. Replace Your Closet Rod
When I'm designing closets, the first thing I look at is the hangers and the rod. Like a good home, you want to address the foundation of the situation. The foundation to a good, well-structured and organized closet begins with these two things in mind. If your closet rod doesn't allow you to seamlessly glide your hanger along the top or is sagging from the weight of your clothes, it needs to be replaced.

For many of us, when we purchase a home, the interior closet has a very inexpensive wire shelf solution with a built-in rod that is stopped every few inches, restricting your ability to move your clothing around. Also, in older homes I've found that the closet rod is very large in diameter and made for old-fashioned hangers. Most hangers are made to fit on a much smaller rod. A new closet buildout doesn't have to be elaborate or expensive to be efficient. This simple adjustment will make your life much easier when you can look at all your clothing without fighting hangers and your closet system.

3. Damaged Clothing
It's important to go through and give your clothing a quick audit. I personally audit my closet every time I go to get dressed, skimming through the items I'm not wearing or are damaged. My lifestyle needs to be flexible, whether I am running around in downtown Seattle or at home on my family farm. My outfits have to be adaptable from casual farm work to Seattle city life.

Even with my farm clothes, if something is damaged, it's a quick and easy decision whether or not it should be removed from my closet. If I purchased something that is now torn or ruined, I give myself the option of either making arrangements to repair it (that week) or recycle it. Remember, you want to have a closet filled with pieces and outfits you love, even if they're just for farm work.

4. Clothing That's Too Small

When you're in the closet, you know what the emotional pieces are because they're at the very end where you don't see them. If you're not trying to lose weight, we have to buy things that will work for you *now.* You are beautiful, and you have to feel good where you are today.

> "I use a three-step process: Cleanse, replenish, and merge. Cleanse is cleaning out the closet. Replenish is finding the right pieces to add to your wardrobe. And merge is bringing your current closet and the new pieces together."
>
> —Tannya Bernadette, Stylist at My Closet Edit

Ladies, ladies, ladies. I don't know why we do this to ourselves. Every woman I've ever known has an area dedicated to "skinny clothes." Give yourself permission to free yourself of clothes that are too small. You want a closet filled with items that fit you right now and make you feel fabulous. Trust me. No matter where you are on the scale, you can feel good about it. We all have skinny clothes. We all need to put a healthy boundary in place for keeping them as well.

My rule of thumb with skinny clothes, especially if your weight tends to fluctuate, is to keep one box of clothing that doesn't currently fit you at the bottom of your closet. My clients will sometimes argue that it's too difficult to downsize their skinny clothes because they're not happy where they are now and want to get back into those clothes. I promise you, if we're talking about downsizing your clothing, chances are, you love to shop and likely will not go back to your skinny box. You may want to wear a few pieces of the past, but you will want to celebrate your future by going on a shopping trip for your new body.

5. Clothing That's Too Big

Again, I'm going to talk to my ladies here. Men, in my experience, don't find it nearly as hard to get rid of clothes as women do. It doesn't matter if they are straight or LGBT+, men tend to not hold such emotional attachment to clothing. Some of us keep our "fat" clothes in fear that we may get big again and have nothing to wear. Fear is such a big motivator in keeping these items.

You don't need to fear your body or how to dress it. Again, if you know that your weight fluctuates, feel free to keep a few things that you love to wear and make you feel good in a box at the bottom of your closet labeled "too big." You may not label this box "fat clothes."

You should just remove the word "fat" from your vocabulary. Only positive feelings are allowed and celebrated in this space. In this space, we will be kind to our bodies and how we dress them.

Ask yourself this: Does everything in my closet make me happy? If you audit your closet this way, eliminating things that are just too big, you can be confident that what you have fits you right now.

Some clients have shared their fear that if they downsize, they won't have much clothing. Great! Who needs a bunch of clothes? It's about quality over quantity. Simplify your clothing routine so that you can go confidently in the direction of who you are, right now, in this space.

Lighting

Do you find yourself frustrated by your closet because it's too dark? Install a motion sensor light. It's an easy and quick fix that will transform the space. Bring light to the darkness. Think of ways you can easily bring light into the situation. Create some ambiance by lighting that dusty candle you've been saving for a special occasion.

Ca$h in on Your Closet

"Hey! I spent a lot of money on that!"
That's what I hear from clients who say they have not and will not ever wear something, but it's staying in the closet "because I spent a fortune on it." The guilt you feel every time you look at it is adding to your emotional clutter. It's like seeing your ex-boyfriend at the grocery store when you have no makeup on. Eek! This is a ghost from your past. You can move to your present by turning it into something of value. An awesome benefit to letting go of your luxury pieces is that you can often consign them for something you'll actually love and wear! If it's hanging in your closet collecting dust, it's not valuable.

A hard spot for many of us is not wanting to get rid of something because we spent a lot of money on it. So many of us are privy to that and feel buyer's remorse. Realistically, this is an opportunity for us to bring them to a business like Zelda Zonk, a boutique consignment shop located in West Seattle.

"I'm a big proponent of only having things in your closet that you really, really love. If you feel good about what you're wearing, it exudes from you. I think of consignment as a place where people can bring the clutter/baggage from their home and give it a new life. Receiving a return on your investment provides ease to suffering from the guilt."

—Jennie McLaughlin, Proprietor, Zelda Zonk Consignment

Online consignment shops such as eBay, ThredUp, and Poshmark make it simple to unload rarely used outfits and make money at the same time.

12 | Taking the Next Steps

Look at your current space and navigate the quickest path to make a dramatic visual change. No matter what you're looking at, if it's a mess (a closet, the kids' toys, an office, the whole house), you can use the Impact Organizing Method to transform it. You now have the framework to ask yourself the right questions to shift your mindset when it comes to acquiring things. If you're looking for a book to tell you what product to buy, this is not the book for you. Let's work with what you have, right where you are.

The issue is not having enough. It's that we live in an American culture of too much. Way too much. Too many decisions, too many distractions, too much stuff.

In my opinion, true success is defined not by what you own but by what you experience and the lives you impact. I'll help you start loving the space you're in and understand that your worth is not determined by your square footage, zip code, or the stuff that fills it.

Awareness + Questions + Method = Successful Outcome!

It's true that everyone and everything demands so much of our time and attention. When it comes to living an organized life, I believe it should be quick and easy. Anyone reading this book can adopt this method and get started today. It doesn't matter if you're hoarding, feel like you're on the verge, or are an aspiring Martha Stewart who just wants to be on the very top of her A-game. This method will change the game for getting your space in order forever.

Making "maybe" piles for later will be a thing of the past. The Impact Organizing Method transforms our relationship with our belongings so that we can learn to live for moments and not things.

13 | The 21-Day Cut the Clutter Challenge

It's widely believed that you can make or break most habits when consistently practicing a routine for twenty-one days. The Society for Personality and Social Psychology found that over forty percent of our everyday actions were not conscious, but habits.

I've seen this advertised everywhere lately. The twenty-one-day mind meditation challenge, the twenty-one-day affirmation challenge, the twenty-one-day fitness challenge...

You may groan at the thought of another challenge. I urge you to look at this challenge through different lenses. If you want to truly cut the clutter out of your life forever, you have to form a new habit of lasting change. You need the right balance of motivation and achievement to keep going. That's why I believe in starting with the twenty-one-day challenge structure. The structure of twenty-one days is proven to jump-start a new habit in your lifestyle. In his best-selling book, Psycho-Cybernetics, Dr. Maxwell Maltz states that, "it requires a minimum of about 21 days for an old mental image to dissolve and a new one to jell."[12]

---

[12] www.Pshyo-Cybernetics.com

This carefully curated challenge will start with the basic fundamentals for forming healthy habits in your mind, your body, your nutrition, and—last, but not least—your relationship with your belongings.

Impact Organizing Challenge

Clutter is the accumulation of stagnant decisions. To cut the clutter, we have to "cycle" out our items. Each item has a cycle. Keeping the flow of items that come into the home must be the same as when they come out of the house. Keeping the cycle consistent is key. Every physical item should have a home and a purpose. Otherwise, it's just clutter. This applies to items that you buy routinely and use on a daily basis. Focus on cycling items that tend to multiply quickly such as bags (paper, plastic, or reusable), clothing, holiday décor, and unused toys.

    My favorite tip of all time for maintaining the clutter on a daily basis is simple and effective. If you do nothing else, this one trick will change the way you look at your possessions. Every time you bring an item into your home, take an item out of your home. I like to leave an empty box marked for donation in my garage at all times. As I'm going through my day looking for things that I no longer need in my life, I simply add them to my donation box. Once the donation box is full, it gets loaded in the car and taken to my favorite charity. Every item in my life has a cycle—a cycle and a purpose. By having this permanent system in my home, the habit of cycling my items is part of my household routine. You also develop a habit of moving room to room and asking what you can part within that particular space.

Are there any items you haven't used in the last year?
Do you honestly need them?

I put my own spin on this challenge. I want you to read the ground rules for the challenge and then start on Day 1. Once you complete Day 1, cross it off your list. That's the only thing you have to do on Day 1. One task, then you're done.

On Day 2, repeat what you did on Day 1, then add the new directions. Cross off Day 2 after you complete it. This is how you work your way down the list—compounding each daily task on top of the previous tasks.

Here are the ground rules for the 21 Day Challenge that will cut the clutter forever:

- Start at Day 1
- Complete each day sequentially and cross off your list.
- Start to compound each day's task into the next day's task.
- Commit to cutting the clutter out of your life forever by completing all twenty-one days.
- If you skip or forget a day, just start with the next day on your list.
- Tell a close friend about your challenge.

You're more likely to stick to your guns if someone else is holding you accountable. In her Fast Company article, Why Sharing Your Progress Makes You More Likely to Accomplish Your Goals, psychologist Elizabeth Lombardo states that accountability is a huge factor in motivating us to cross items off our lists. When no one is around to say anything about an incomplete task, Lombardo argues, it's easy to push it to the next day, then the next week, and so on.

- Want to get social? Share your journey using the hashtag #ImpactOrganizingMethod

- Be kind to yourself and know that at times it may be hard. This is a challenge for a reason!
- Have fun and feel the sense of accomplishment as you complete the task for the day.
- Our 21-Day Impact Organizing Challenge starts with our internal and moves to the external areas of your life.

*"What I know for sure:
Our internal space has to be given the same level of respect and diligent attention as the external."
—Oprah Winfrey*

Day 1: Make Your Bed
Upon opening your eyes in the morning, get up and out of bed. Then make it. Making your bed each morning may seem like the least of your worries. However, according to Admiral William McRaven, it may be the best way to start off your day. If you make your bed every morning, you'll have accomplished the first task of the day. It will give you a small sense of pride and encourage you to do another task—then another and another. By the end of the day, that one task completed will have turned into many tasks completed. Making your bed will also reinforce the fact that little things in life matter.

Day 2: Change Your Morning Routine
Breaking a negative pattern, such as checking your email first thing in the morning, dramatically changes your entire day. I like to start my morning off with ten minutes of stretching and ten minutes of meditation. If I'm not mindful, I can't create my ideal morning.

When I'm not setting my intention for the day, my old habits will just kick in and do it for me. I'll immediately get on Facebook, Instagram, Snapchat, and Pinterest before I hit up my email without really thinking about it! In a blink, I'll still be lying in bed an hour later and have done nothing for myself but fill my mind with outside thoughts and perceptions. The only thing that bad habit does is cloud your mind. Change your morning routine to be intentional, and you will change your life.

Day 3: The Real Beauty of Sleep
Sleep is a thing of beauty if done right. The lack of sleep can make you grumpy all day, but a good night of sleep will keep you energized all day. Going to bed and waking up at the same time every day is crucial. "Your body likes predictability," says neuroscientist Jordan Gaines Lewis in Psychology Today. Many smartphones offer a sleep time app that lets you set the wake-up time, key in the number of hours you'd like to sleep, and set the nights you'd like reminders. The app will alert you before your bedtime to let you know what time you're supposed to be tucked in to get your full night's rest. If you have to get up each morning at seven thirty and want to get eight solid hours of shut eye, your bedtime needs to be eleven thirty at night. It's as simple as that.

All successful individuals are strict with this golden rule. I don't know about you, but I love my bed. I love naps, I love my mattress, I love my pillows, I love my sheets... It's my safe place. If you don't love your bed, you probably won't get good rest. It's crucial to get good sleep so you can be ready for the day.

Day 4: Get Used to Feeling Uncomfortable
We as an American society have gotten too comfortable with being comfortable! You're going to be okay. Forming a new habit of less may feel uncomfortable at first. You can be crabby—it's okay, you've got this. It will take a little time to get comfortable with it. Taking full responsibility of your life doesn't always feel good. It's called auditing, and sometimes it can really suck.

But if you want to conquer the chaos and cut the clutter for good, it needs to start here. You'll soon feel that everything is temporary and doesn't need to be comforted by stuff. Learn to let the urges pass.
They're like clouds in the sky drifting in the wind.

Day 5: What do You Need Today?
You are your most important asset you own. Put yourself back on top of your priority list. Taking care of everyone else and disregarding your own personal needs can only lead to a stressful and chaotic environment. Just like the flight attendants advise before takeoff, put your own face mask on first before helping others—even children.

I've worked with so many mothers who greet me with an apology. They haven't had time to take a shower because they are so busy. Being good to yourself first. (Go take a shower, girl!) Your current environment is a reflection of where you are now, not where your life could be. Without a healthy, happy you, there isn't a home. Just a house longing for warmth and life. Give yourself a compliment today. Be kind to yourself today.

Day 6: Practice Organized Thinking
Declutter your thoughts by creating a brain dump as shown in the previous chapter. Get it out of your head and onto paper. Starting each day with a quick brain dump is so important for staying focused on what you truly want to accomplish for the day.

Day 7: Positive Communication
When difficult situations arise, find the positive. It's all too easy to blame others and find the negative in any situation. Rise above it. Think, seek, and speak positively.

Day 8: Brain food, Not Butt Food

Start a healthy diet. Eating smart foods helps maintain a positive frame of mind. If you're in the car often, always stock water and pack smart snacks. Leave them in the car for when you get the hunger bug. When you can think clearly and positively, you can begin to make rational decisions rather than emotional ones.

Getting rid of clutter takes mental preparation. If you're sleepy and undernourished, making decisions becomes challenging. Take care of yourself and fuel yourself with the good stuff so you can make decisions from a healthy place. You'll also notice it will be easier to make decisions more quickly. The quicker you are at making decisions and taking action, the bigger impact you will have.

Day 9: Practice Gratitude
Give thanks for all that you have, right here in this current moment.

Gratitude increases mental strength. For years, research has shown gratitude not only reduces stress, but it may also play a major role in overcoming trauma. A 2006 study published in Behavior Research and Therapy found that Vietnam War Veterans with higher levels of gratitude experienced lower rates of post-traumatic stress disorder. A 2003 study published in the Journal of Personality and Social Psychology found that gratitude was a major contributor to resilience following the terrorist attacks on September 11. Recognizing all you have to be thankful for, even during the worst times of your life, fosters resilience.

We all have the ability and opportunity to cultivate gratitude. Take a few moments to focus on all that you have rather than complain about all the things you think you deserve.

Day 10: Get Outside
We were not created to sit inside brick buildings, stare at screens under florescent lights for hours each day, then to get

into a mobile metal box to arrive in a house and fall asleep in a space filled with stuff. We've got to get out!

Embracing nature will help to eliminate stress and get your ideas flowing. Everything outside is living. The trees, the fish in the stream, the grass, and even the bugs in the ground. Everything is thriving and surviving outside. Being in creation will allow your senses to come alive. It's so easy to get lost in the day to day. If you can, take a moment to walk around your neighborhood or go to a park and enjoy a quick little nature walk. Your soul will thank you.

Notice how you feel when you arrive back home. How does your home feel? Cozy and warm? Stressful and cold? Now you can identify the areas that need improvement with a different and fresh perspective.

Day 11: Drop Spot
We already talked about creating consistency with drop spots. Think about items you use on a daily basis, like your keys, mail, purse, glasses. Create drop spots for these items so that you always place the item in the same spot. When items have a consistent home, you don't spend time looking for them. You know where to find everything, and they don't end up cluttering up areas they don't belong!

Day 12: Pick Up After Yourself
Say what? I know.
We've been told this so many times in our life, we feel like we've gotten a free pass as adults. But how's that working for you? If you open it, close it. If you pull it out, put it back. This applies to everything you touch.

Day 13: Save Money
When it comes to clutter, it's usually the accumulation of everything you've purchased with your hard-earned money. Instead, I want you to take all the money you would have spent

on impulse buys and accumulate some money in your savings account! Next time you want to grab that instinct item, grab your phone and transfer the value of the item to your savings account. It's the exact money you would have spent going straight into your savings!

Day 14: Eliminate
Choose something to eliminate or donate from your home. Choose anything, big or small. My golden rule for everyday clutter is that everything that goes in must come out. Doesn't matter what it is, even if it's groceries. You bring it in, then something has to go out. Now. Try giving your home a quick clean sweep for any items that haven't been used this year—or any year! If you haven't used it in the last year, you don't need it, you didn't need it, and you won't need it.

Day 15: Donation Bin
Centralize donation areas in your home. I like to have one in my closet and in my garage for easy discarding. Every time I try something on that doesn't fit or make me feel confident, I put it straight into my donate bin. Once it's filled, I take it to a charity like The Children's Home Society of Washington. Form a habit of cycling your items out of your home when they no longer serve you. The beauty of having a dedicated donation bin is that you're helping someone else who would love to have those items. Keep what you love and give what you don't to someone else.

Day 16: Rock Your Power Outfit
Every outfit you own should make you feel good. By choosing the outfit the night before, you can save precious morning time for exercise or hugs with your kids. Set out all your clothes (undergarments. too) as well as any accessories you will wear with your outfit. Enlist your children to do the same. This will

spare you the inevitable morning argument about who wears what.

Day 17: Get Your Paperwork Under Control

Understand your organizing style and design a filing system that's easy for you to maintain. The "right way" is the easiest way for you to maintain it. That's the difference between failure and success when creating a filing system.

Choose a cluttered surface and put all paperwork in one pile. Start at the top and complete or file each piece of paperwork one at a time.

Every year reassess, your home filing system and purge unnecessary documents. Contain your notes, lists, and ideas in one notebook. Those sticky notes decorating your computer station are chaos to your mind! Keep it all centralized and focused.

Day 18: Focus on Creating Space, Rather Than Filling It

Once you start purging, your space may look different or even bare. It's okay to have empty drawers and spaces. Not every space needs to be filled with stuff. Create some breathing room.

Why do you think you feel so peaceful when you get away to a nice hotel? You have all the amenities you need minus all the clutter! You can create a new space simply by not filling it with stuff. Stop wandering the aisles of HomeGoods to fill every corner. Focus on key pieces you love, then create clean and clear surface spaces.

Day 19: Don't Forget the Car

If I were to ask you for a ride to the store right now, how would you react? Would you be clearing the seat of garbage, throwing clothes and toys to the back? Treat this environment like you would your office. Keep it clean, organized, and free of excess waste.

Day 20: Garbage and Recycle
Get rid of all visible, obvious garbage from every room. Start at the front door and work your way room to room with trash bag in hand. In most cases, I've found that by removing all the visible garbage and breaking down all those wonderful Amazon boxes, you get a huge chunk of your space back. Things like bags of bags (paper or plastic) tend to pile up easily. Do a quick sweep of your spaces and focus on getting rid of the garbage and recycling.

Day 21: Social Media Detox
I know you may be taking all kinds of super cute selfies with your #ImpactOrganizingMethod progress, but I do want to offer this challenge. Twenty-four hours with no social media.

Social media contributes to anxiety and depression in all sorts of different ways. The more we consume, the more problems it can cause. Researchers have even created a scale called The Bergen Facebook Addiction Scale to measure this behavior. A study out of the University of Michigan has found that people who use Facebook routinely are more likely to be unhappy than people who use it less. Those avid users also said they were less satisfied with their lives overall. This could be because people often compare their real lives to idealized versions of their friends' lives online.

Don't compare, just share. Let's retrain our brain and empty this clutter from our mind.

This is a challenge. It's supposed to be challenging! But it can be done, little by little, each and every day. I hope you enjoyed your 21-Day Impact Organizing Challenge and that you now realize you can get more out of your life by living with less.

14 | Make an Impact

Thank you so much, I'm honored you took the time to read this book and that my experience has become a part of your journey to living with less and making an impact. I know how truly rewarding the benefits of living with less can be. It doesn't have to take a lifetime to get organized. You just need the right roadmap.

Getting organized doesn't have to take forever. With my Impact Organizing Method, you can transform any space in a single day. The level of organizing may vary, but you will not waste time in a black-hole box of miscellaneous stuff. Focusing on the bigger picture and organizing for an impactful difference can be life changing. We also dived into the high price of clutter and looked at what it's really costing you. So many aspects of your life are affected by clutter, including your personal and professional relationships, work life, and finances.

Clutter is aggressive and often has an insidious way of seeping into so many areas of our lives. It's amazing to look at all that can open up in your life when you simply declare you will cut the clutter once and for all.

Of course, it's hard to focus on any one task when your mind is running amok. I've had clients just stare at me and say, "I can't even think right now. I have too much on my mind to even know where to start." That's why we put the discussion of decluttering your mind in the first part of this book. When you've got your mind right, you step into the driver's seat of your life. Letting thoughts and clutter control you are a thing of the past.

Creating an organized home from top to bottom becomes so much easier when you understand that there's a blueprint for how to do it. You no longer have to feel overwhelmed, not knowing where to start when you're drowning in clutter. Breaking it down into bite-sized action steps makes it attainable, and you can see results in real time. Positive self-talk and self-care go hand in hand with living an organized life.

A quick project like getting rid of five things in your closet is a great place to start. This is something easy to tackle in thirty minutes or less. You never understand the real weight clutter has on your life until you're consumed by it. We broke down some key areas in your life where you may be carrying weight you didn't know you could lose simply by decluttering your life.

Clutter may find a way to distract from the beauty of our lives, but we can turn all of that around by cultivating a clutter-free confidence.

No matter where you are on your journey, just keep going.
Will you have setbacks?
Sure.
Life happens, and we must be prepared to brave the storm.

You can make a life worth fighting for—a life that's exciting to come home to. Even among the most devastating moments in life, there's always beauty. Seek it. Trust that tomorrow is a new day to start over. Nourish yourself with whatever brings joy to your soul.

Watching the Oprah Winfrey Show in the middle of life's chaos changed my life, all because I saw a man named Peter Walsh help others in a way I'd never seen before.

Oprah's show gave me the confidence every week to "live my best life" and motivated me to start a business off creating a few simple posts on Craigslist.

At just twenty-one years old, I was organizing complete strangers' homes for just one hundred dollars a day. Fast-forward a decade later—you're reading a book written by that same girl.

A girl from a small town of McKenna, Washington—the girl with a dream who always seemed to be in the middle of chaos. If I can do this, I know without a shred of doubt that you can, too.

Live your life with less so that you can have more of everything that matters most.

I Got it from My Momma

Do you ever catch yourself doing something exactly the way your mom does it? I'm guilty. There are some habits that must be genetic.

I fold towels just like my mom does.

Ever walk into someone's bathroom to find the towels perfectly folded? That was my mom's house. You know she had been somewhere by the folded towels.

Even though I've been out of contact with her for nearly a decade, I still have her moves, her traits, and her mannerisms running through my every day. As an adult, when I sit down to fold my towels just as she did, it's a soulful moment of connection—a silent, automatic prayer. It's a small moment of gratitude, remembering every time throughout my childhood she would pull warm sheets from the dryer and throw them over me. How we would sit in front of the TV and perfectly fold each towel's corners to a point, lay it onto a flat

surface, then fold it into thirds before one final pat.
That's how my mama does it.
That technique, that trait, that memory—has been used for folding towels in thousands of Seattle homes.
Because I do it like my mama.
I urge you to have fun with this question.
What do you do just like your _____ (*insert a loved one*)

Share your answers on social media using
#impactorganizingmethod

My Wish

I hope that you will share the Impact Organizing Method with someone who's struggling with getting their home organized. I've created this book as an introduction and step-by-step process for those who are looking to simplify their lives and overcome the burden of clutter. If you know of someone who could benefit from these teachings, please share it. I've often gone into clients' homes who have shared with me that a friend or family member has given them a book on organizing that encouraged them to reach out and ask for help. Letting someone know they are not alone is such a tremendous gift. I hope this book brings some laughter, light, and love to all those who read it.

Remember that you can make an impact right where you're at.

Whatever dream you may have for your life; you can start or pick back up right where you are. Anything telling you otherwise; is just clutter.

About The Author

Author, Entrepreneur, creator of The Organizing Experts and former Seattle Seahawks NFL cheerleader, Kammie Lisenby has dedicated her life to helping others find peace and purpose. She's guided hundreds of families through lifechanging transformations using the Impact Organizing Method.

When Kammie's not organizing, you can find her at Lisenby Farm—an eleven-acre plot of inherited wonderland she's remodeled into a magical Pacific Northwest retreat. Aside from being named "Seattle's Favorite Organizing Expert" by the Seattle Home Remodel Show, she has also been featured on OWN Network, King5 News, New Day Northwest, O, The Oprah Magazine, and Seattle Homes & Lifestyle.

Visit http://www.organizingexperts.com

Social Media @OrganizingExperts & @KammieLisenby

Acknowledgements

I'd like to thank a few special families, teachers, mentors, and individuals who have made an *impact* on my life.

Ida Mae Lisenby, I know what it means to be loved unconditionally because I have had the blessing of the world's most doting gramma. I thank you every day, for the many sacrifices you've made to insure I can always, come home.

Stephen Leroy Lisenby, a force to be reckoned with. Because of you, I am a Lisenby. Thank you for teaching me the value of character, appreciation, hard work and compassion.

Alice Irene Lisenby, my mother, I love you. You are never far from my heart and thoughts.

Jessica Reeves Clark and Judy Edwards without your love, support, friendship and (editing help) this book would not be possible.
Britnee Rogich, my best friend, soul sister and biggest cheerleader thank you and I love you. Bryann, BreLena and Kabenzie Kalinski, Zuzu and Sabyne Hanson, having you next door all those years was a saving grace to my life.

Elizabeth Sherman, my rock, my soul sister, I cannot thank you enough for your unconditional love and support. You are my Northstar.

Jenell Thompson, Sandy Wehnes, Shannon French, John & Rae Ebsary, Liz and David Kelley, your friendship and companionship means the world to me.

Matthew James Wilson, I love you and thank you for all your support.

To the families who allowed this girl to sleep on their couch, got me through high school and took me in as their own.

The Sherman family, The Sartain family, The Youngchild family, The Haakenson family, Amber Mayerl and family, Richelle Kimball and family, Gina & Jim Torgerson and Frances Clark.

To the mentors who changed the trajectory of my life.

Oprah Winfrey, Peter Walsh, Ali Brown, Marie Forleo, Tanya Albert, Mr. Laforest, Mr. Coffing and the best damn dance teacher Angela Collins Mitchell.

To my clients who have loved and supported my small business.

Susan Silver, Jessica Eaves Mathews, Liz Castro, Therese O'Niell, Cynamon Quinton & Mary Kay Bowman. Your grace, leadership and ability to persevere has been a blessing to be a part of. Thank you for allowing me into your home and family. It's been my absolute pleasure.

Resources Recommended By The Author

Real Estate
Ashley Lisenby of John L. Scott
(Vashon, WA)
https://ashleylisenby.johnlscott.com/

Personal Wardrobe Stylist
Tannya Bernadette (Seattle, WA)
https://myclosetedit.com/

Styled Seattle (Seattle, WA)
https://www.styledseattle.com/

Hoarding Help
Bio Decon Solutions – Scott Barkley
https://biodeconsolutions.com/

Nutrition
Sarah Adler of Simply Real Health
https://simplyrealhealth.com/

Tiny Home Builder
Kurt Galley of Carriage Houses NW
http://carriagehousesnw.com/

Business Coaching
Ali Brown
https://alibrown.com/

Marie Forleo
https://www.marieforleo.com/

BIO DECON SOLUTIONS

24 HOUR EMERGENCY RESPONSE

I'm Scott Barkley, owner of Bio Decon Solutions . My experience and history in various hospital and correctional settings has allowed me to honE my skillset to provide help and solutions for those who are struggling with home hoarding and clean up. Bio Decon Solutions helps individuals with compassion and discretion. We help individuals and families clean up:

HOARDING
UNATTENDED DEATHS
SUICIDES
HOMICIDES
HOMELESS CAMPS
SQUATTERS

(253) 320-8657 | WWW.BIODECONSOLUTIONS.COM

Organizing Experts

Do you have a small business or home brand you'd like to showcase?

We are looking for brand partnerships that make an impact.

For more information on brand partnership opportunities

CONTACT US

OrganizingExperts.com/Media
Info@OrganizingExperts.com

Made in the USA
Las Vegas, NV
19 March 2021